T0227642

Excel 97 for Windows®
Made Simple

Stephen Morris

Routledge
Taylor & Francis Group

LONDON AND NEW YORK

First published 1997 by Made Simple

2 Park Square, Milton Park, Abingdon, Oxon OX14 4RN
711 Third Avenue, New York, NY 10017, USA

Routledge is an imprint of the Taylor & Francis Group, an informa business

First issued in hardback 2017

British Library Cataloguing in Publication Data
A catalogue record for this book is available from the British Library

ISBN 978-0-7506-3802-9 (pbk)
ISBN 978-1-138-43625-1 (hbk)

Typeset by Butford Technical Publishing, Bodenham, Hereford
Archetype, Bash Casual, Cotswold and Gravity fonts from Advanced Graphics Ltd
Icons designed by Sarah Ward © 1994

Transferred to digital print 2009

Contents

Preface

Excel 97 is the latest in a long line of spreadsheet applications that has seen this grid-based software evolve from a simple number-crunching tool into a sophisticated data management and reporting environment.

Excel 97 is part of the Office 97 suite and, as such, is tightly integrated with the other programs in the package. As a consequence, reports and charts produced in Excel can be based on an Access database and transferred into a Word document or PowerPoint presentation in seconds.

This version of Excel has a number of enhancements over previous editions and, as a result, the system requirements for running the software are considerably more arduous than for its predecessors. Office 97 demands a minimum of a 486 computer with 8 Mb of memory and 73 Mb of hard-disk space (much more if you want to install the entire suite). Excel 97 runs only under Windows 95 or Windows NT.

This book aims to provide new users of Excel 97 with the information needed to get started with the program. No previous spreadsheet knowledge is required but it is assumed that the reader can perform the standard Windows tasks, such as clicking and dragging.

The fundamental aspects of Excel are covered in some detail and will give the reader a thorough grounding in the software and its operation. It should then be possible to build on this knowledge in order to make use of Excel's more sophisticated features. With a little practice, the most useful facilities are quickly mastered and Excel 97 can be applied to the processing of complex data sets and the production of professional-looking reports.

Acknowledgements

I would like to thank Microsoft Corporation for their assistance while this book was in preparation.

Thanks also to Emily Morris for typesetting the book.

1 The main principles

Introducing Excel 97

The Excel spreadsheet program is designed to make the manipulation of information easy and fast. The program can process many types of data: from mainly numeric tables – such as balance sheets, sales returns and production schedules – to the sort of lists more usually associated with database programs. This book will show you how these various types of information can be handled.

Starting up

To get Excel up and running, follow these steps:

1 Click on the Windows 95 Start button, in the bottom left-hand corner of the screen.

2 Select the Programs option.

3 Select Microsoft Excel from the list.

The program is loaded and the Excel display will take up most of the screen.

Alternatively, if you have created an Office 97 folder on the desktop, double-click on the Excel icon.

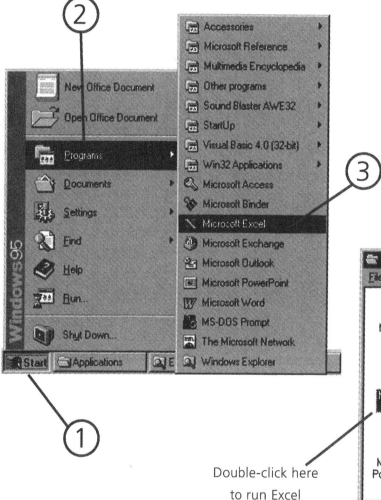

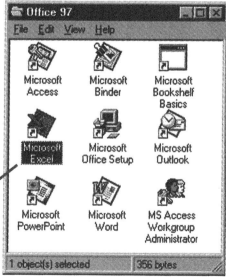

Double-click here to run Excel

In the Office Assistant:

- Click on either of the first two options in the 'bubble' to get more detailed information.

- Click on the Assistant's title bar to see more options.

For more information on Excel's help facilities, see page 8.

The first time you run Excel, the **Office Assistant** is displayed. This animated picture can provide help in a number of ways that may be attractive for new users, though existing users are likely to find it extremely irritating.

If you want to get straight into Excel, click on 'Start using Microsoft Excel', then click on the Assistant's close button.

Take note

If you close down the Office Assistant, it will not appear the next time you run Excel. However, you can always bring it back to life by selecting Microsoft Excel Help from the Help menu or clicking on the Office Assistant toolbar button.

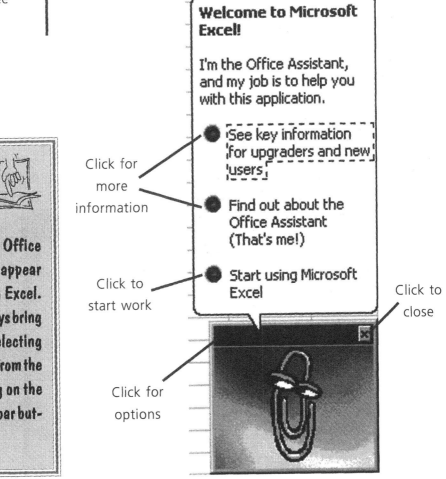

Welcome to Microsoft Excel!

I'm the Office Assistant, and my job is to help you with this application.

See key information for upgraders and new users

Find out about the Office Assistant (That's me!)

Start using Microsoft Excel

Click for more information

Click to start work

Click for options

Click to close

Screen components

The guiding principle behind Windows is supposed to be that it makes computer applications easier to use. Certainly the use of a mouse for selecting options is preferable to the complicated key-based commands that had to be memorised for older applications, and the use of icons and buttons with simple pictures on them can make the choice of actions easier. However, Excel 97, in common with most Windows 95 applications, provides a screen that is extremely cluttered and can be very daunting to the new user. The screen contains all the usual Windows features.

- ☐ The **control menu** leads to the standard Windows menu.

- ☐ The **title bar** is used to move the window.

- ☐ The **minimise button** converts the window to an icon.

- ☐ The **maximise button** makes the window full size.

- ☐ The **close button** closes down the program.

- ☐ Dragging the corners and edges changes the window size.

Control menu: click for Windows menu

Title bar: drag to move window

Minimise button: click to convert to icon

Maximise button: window is initially full size

Close button: click to end program

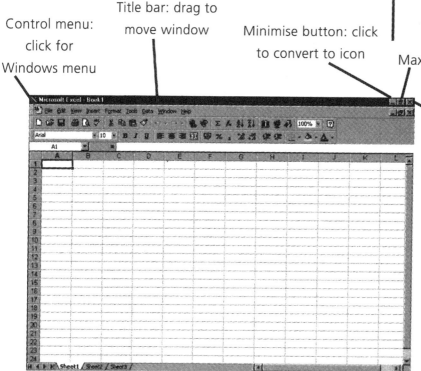

- The **menu bar** has a set of drop-down menus that provide access to all of Excel's features.

- The **toolbar** is a double row of buttons and selection boxes which, in most cases, provide shortcuts to the menu options or quick ways of entering values.

- The **tab buttons** and **sheet tabs** let you move from one worksheet to another.

- The **scroll bars** allow fast movement within a sheet.

- The **status bar** is used by Excel for displaying messages and giving information, such as whether the **[Num Lock]** and **[Caps Lock]** keys are switched on.

- The **title bar** tells you the title of the file.

- The main **grid** is where data is entered and results are displayed.

The main components of the display are listed briefly here, with fuller descriptions given later.

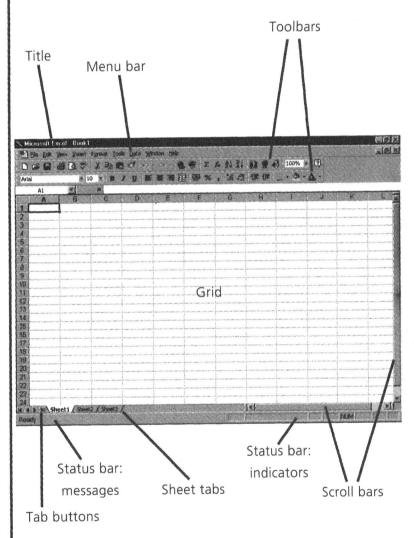

5

The worksheet grid

In common with all other spreadsheet programs, Excel is organised around a simple grid system. The grid consists of a rectangular array of rows and columns and is called a **worksheet**. The columns are labelled with letters: A, B, C and so on; the rows are numbered from 1 down the sheet.

The intersection of each row and column forms a **cell**. Any item of data entered on the sheet is placed in one of these cells; each cell can hold one and only one item of data.

The cells are identified by combining the cell letter and row number. For example, the cell in the top left-hand corner of the sheet is A1. To the right of this is B1, then C1, and so on. The cells in the second row are labelled A2, B2, C2 etc.

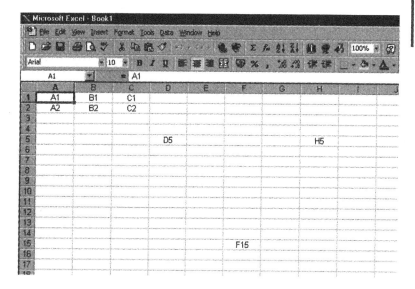

Limits

Excel allows you to create very large worksheets.

☐ The first 26 columns are labelled A to Z, the next 26 are AA to AZ, then BA to BZ, and so on up to column IV (giving 256 columns in all).

☐ The rows are numbered from 1 to 65,536, giving over 16 million cells.

However, spreadsheets become unmanageable if they get too large.

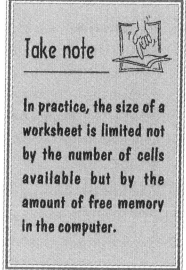

Take note

In practice, the size of a worksheet is limited not by the number of cells available but by the amount of free memory in the computer.

Moving around the sheet

□ Click on the scroll bar arrows to move the display one row or column at a time.

□ Click on the grey scroll areas to move by one screenful in any direction.

□ Drag the buttons on the scroll bars to move by large amounts.

□ Click on a cell to make it active.

□ Use the cursor keys to make an adjacent cell active.

□ Press **[F5]** and enter a new cell reference to make any cell on the sheet active.

The main difficulty with any spreadsheet program is that you can only ever see a small proportion of the worksheet at any one time. There are scroll bars to the right and below the grid, which allow you to move around the worksheet.

One cell is always **active**. This is the cell where data can be entered (initially A1). The active cell is identified by a thicker border. Any cell can be made the active cell by using the arrow keys, clicking on a cell or selecting a new cell with the menu options. Only one cell can be active at a time.

Reference of current cell

Active cell

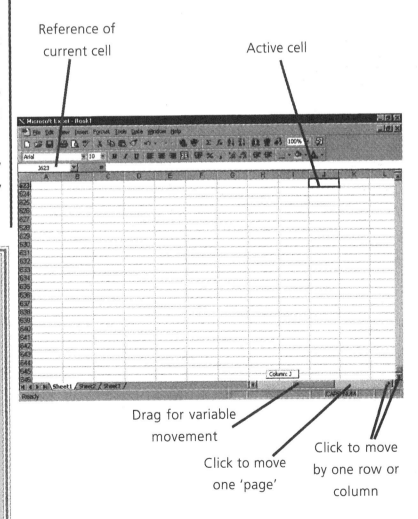

Drag for variable movement

Click to move one 'page'

Click to move by one row or column

Take note

As you drag the scroll bar buttons, a pop-up label tells you what row will be at the top of the window or what column will be on the left when you release the button.

7

Getting help

Excel provides a dazzling range of on-screen help options, offering step-by-step help on every subject and a vast range of hints and tips. The best way to learn about Excel's help facilities is by experience but the many options available can be confusing at first.

The **Help menu** leads to a traditional Windows help program, and has links to the Office Assistant, the Internet and help for Lotus 1-2-3 users.

The **Office Assistant** lets you type in direct questions and then lists help topics that may match the text you have entered. The Assistant also displays tips based on your actions.

Labels are displayed under the toolbar buttons if you rest the pointer over them.

The **status bar** gives instructions when you select a menu option.

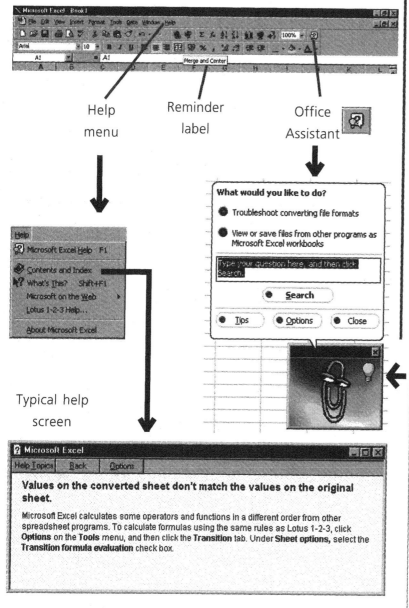

Help menu

Reminder label

Office Assistant

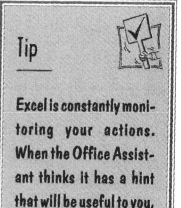

Typical help screen

Options

- Clicking on the close button, choosing Close from the control menu or pressing **[Alt]+[F4]** ends the program.

- Selecting Exit from the File menu (or **[Alt] [F] [X]**) also closes the program.

- Clicking on the minimise button reduces Excel to an icon; the program and worksheet remain in memory.

- Clicking on another window pushes Excel to the back of the display without closing it down.

- **[Alt]+[Tab]** and **[Alt]+ [Esc]** provide alternative methods of selecting other applications without closing Excel.

You can get out of Excel 97 – either permanently or temporarily – using any of the usual Windows 95 methods.

- If you close Excel down, then you will have to reload the worksheet at the start of your next session (or begin a new worksheet). Loading is described on page 25.

- If you temporarily move to some other Windows 95 application, the current worksheet will be maintained in memory (but do save it first, just in case – see page 20).

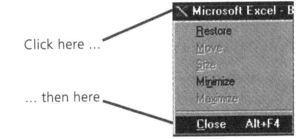

Click here ...

... then here

OR:

Click here ...

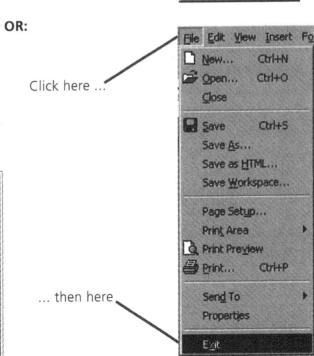

... then here

Take note

If you try to close Excel without saving your work, you will be prompted to do so.

Summary of Section 1

- Excel 97 is loaded from within Windows 95 in the same way as any other application.

- Data is entered onto a **worksheet**, which consists of a grid of individual **cells**.

- Columns are labelled with letters, from A to Z, AA to IV.

- Rows are numbered from 1 to 65,536.

- One cell is **active** at any time. A different cell can be made active by clicking on it; other areas of the worksheet can be viewed using the scroll bars.

- Help comes in the form of a Help menu, the Office Assistant, help buttons, reminder labels and status bar.

- The File menu, control menu and close button provide all the usual Windows 95 methods for leaving Excel 97 (either temporarily or permanently).

2 Creating a worksheet

Entering data

Excel always starts with a blank worksheet. Entering data is simply a matter of selecting a cell and then typing a value. You can enter numbers or text in any cell. As an example, create a worksheet with this simple table:

	A	B	C	D	E
1					
2		TOTAL SALES: NORTH			
3					
4			1997	1996	% Change
5		1st Qtr	1092	1048	
6		2nd Qtr	718	623	
7		3rd Qtr	1953	1955	
8		4th Qtr	908	705	
9		TOTAL			

Start by entering the labels around the main block of data:

1 Click on cell B2 so that it is the active cell.

2 Type **TOTAL SALES: NORTH**. As you do so, the text appears in the cell and, simultaneously, in the formula bar, above the column labels.

3 Press **[Enter]** when the text is complete. The cursor moves down to the next cell.

4 Now click on C4 to enter **1997**, and D4 for **1996**.

5 Enter **% Change** in E4.

Take note

Excel recognises most of the entries as text and places them on the left of the cell. However, it treats 1996 and 1997 as numbers, putting them on the right of the cells. These values will be changed to text later.

Tip

You can also complete an entry by pressing one of the cursor keys or clicking on another cell.

6 Enter the row titles in cells B5 to B9. (Here, you do not need to click on the cells below B5 because the cursor moves down when you press **[Enter]**.)

7 Click on C5 and enter the value **1092**.

8 Fill in the other seven values in the cells from C6 to C8 and D5 to D8.

The totals will be calculated by the system when a formula is entered (see page 28).

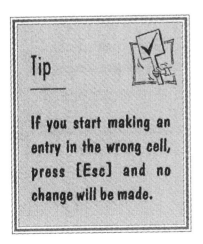

Tip

If you start making an entry in the wrong cell, press [Esc] and no change will be made.

Excel will always try to decide for itself what sort of data is being entered:

● If the value starts with a number, + or – sign, and contains only numeric characters, it is treated as a numeric value.

● If the entry begins with a + or – sign (with letters) or an = sign, Excel assumes it is a formula.

● If the value starts with any other character, Excel assumes the entry is a piece of text.

Numeric values and the results of numeric formulae are always aligned on the right-hand side of the columns. By default, text entries are placed on the left.

Formula bar

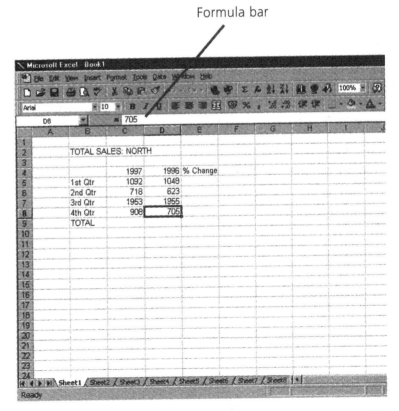

Text and number formats

If you want a numeric value to be treated as text, start by typing an apostrophe ('). This is a special code to indicate a text value and will not be displayed in the cell.

Excel assumes that a non-numeric entry is text, so there is no need to use the apostrophe except where there might otherwise be confusion:

- When the entry looks like a number

- When the entry starts with =, + or – but is not a formula

- When you want a real apostrophe to be displayed at the start of the label (start by typing **two** apostrophes).

To change the **1997** and **1996** labels to text:

1 Click on C4.

2 Type **'1997** and press **[Enter]**.

3 Click on D4.

4 Type **'1996** and press **[Enter]**.

Take note

It is important to make the distinction between text and numeric entries, especially if you intend to use the contents of cells in a formula. Excel will not allow you to mix text and numbers in the same formula without using a special function. So if you want to add two numbers together, they must both be entered as numbers; and if you want to combine two pieces of text (for instance, combine 'January' with '1997' to make 'January 1997'), the value '1997' must have been entered as text, with an apostrophe in front.

Tip

You can also centre a title in a row so that it stretches over several columns – see page 74.

Numbers

The type of display depends on the numeric value:

☐ Whole numbers (**integers**) are displayed with no decimal point (e.g. 123).

☐ **Decimals** are shown with as many decimal places as are needed, and with a zero to the left of the decimal point for numbers less than 1 (e.g. 12.3, 1.23, 0.123, 0.0123).

☐ Very large and very small numbers are given in **Scientific** format (e.g. 1.23E+09) – see page 62.

☐ If the cell is too narrow to show a complete number, it is filled with # marks (though the number is still safely held in memory).

Numbers are displayed using the **General** format, unless you specify otherwise. With this format, Excel selects the most appropriate style in each individual case, using the least number of decimal places possible (and none at all for whole numbers).

In many cases this leads to an untidy display and you will want to change the format; details of how to do this are given in Section 7.

	Integers	Decimals	Exponential		Narrow column
	1	1.2	6E+19		#####
	32	4.708	2.304E+11		#####
	623	2.94571	3.462E+13		#####
	1752	0.23	4E-10		#####
	22385468	0.00004	6.23E-14		#####

Take note

You can apply different formats to individual cells or groups of cells. For instance, you can put a monetary symbol in front of money amounts or separate thousands with commas – see Section 7. You can also design your own format – see page 68.

Simple editing

If you make a mistake, it's easily put right; there's no need to start all over again. The contents of any cell can be replaced or revised with very little effort.

Displayed value temporarily truncated during editing

Editing cursor

Formula bar

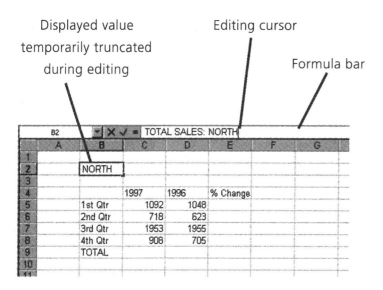

To edit the contents of a cell:

1 Click on the cell that contains the incorrect value. The value or formula appears in the formula bar.

2 To replace the value altogether, just type a new entry; there's no need to delete the existing value.

3 To change the value, click on the formula bar. Use the cursor keys or mouse to position the cursor within the value, then use the **[Delete]** key to erase the character to the right of the cursor or the **[Backspace]** key to delete to the left. New characters can be inserted at the cursor position.

You can also edit in the cell itself by double-clicking on the cell.

Tip

You can use the Windows cut-and-paste facilities to transfer text between applications. For example, [Ctrl]+[V] pastes text from the clipboard into the current cell; [Ctrl]+[C] copies the contents of the current cell or highlighted text from the formula bar; [Ctrl]+[X] deletes the contents of a cell or highlighted text and places a copy in the clipboard. Clipboard data can be inserted into any appropriate Windows application.

Basic steps

To delete the contents of a cell:

1 Click on the cell.
2 Press the **[Delete]** key. (This is a shortcut for the Edit | Clear | All command.)

If you realise a mistake is being made as you are entering data, you can press **[Esc]** to abandon the entry. Whatever was in the cell beforehand is unaffected.

However, if a wrong entry has been made, or the contents of a cell are no longer needed, it can be deleted.

Mistakes can usually be cancelled, even after completing an entry, by pressing **[Ctrl]+[Z]**. This Undo action restores the original contents of the last cell changed and can be used after editing, replacing or deleting the contents of a cell. Each time you press **[Ctrl]+[Z]**, another action is cancelled.

You can undo several actions at once by clicking on the Undo list button on the toolbar. The list shows the most recent actions and any that you mark are cancelled.

Similarly, the Redo options repeat actions that have been cancelled by Undo.

Most recent actions to be undone

Undo last action

Undo list

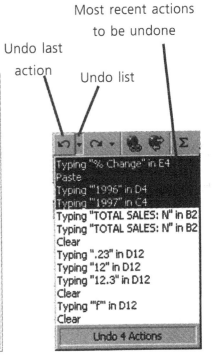

Take note

There is another way that is often used to blank out a cell: click on the cell, press the space bar and press [Enter]. However, this can cause problems in formulae that refer to the cell. Excel replaces the contents of the cell with a piece of text consisting of a single space and any attempt to include this in a numeric formula results in an error. Therefore, this method of 'blanking out' cells should be avoided.

Summary of Section 2

❑ Data is typed directly into the cells.

❑ Excel decides whether each entry is text or numeric data; text is placed on the left of the cell, numbers on the right.

❑ Numbers and formulae can be treated as text by typing an apostrophe (') at the front of the text.

❑ Numeric values are displayed in the **General** format, with no more decimal places than are needed, and none at all for whole numbers (integers).

❑ To edit data, click on the cell, then retype or use the editing keys.

❑ To delete data, click on the cell, then press **[Delete]**.

❑ To cancel an action, press **[Ctrl]+[Z]**. Use the Undo buttons to cancel a series of actions and Redo to restore cancellations.

3 File operations

Saving the worksheet

It is essential to get into the habit of saving your work regularly. The data you have entered so far exists only in the computer's memory and it will be lost unless you save it in a file before leaving Excel.

The worksheet data may also be lost if the program – or Windows – crashes (i.e. produces a fatal error message that results in the application being forcibly closed). This does not happen often but when it does, it's usually at the most inconvenient moment! So, save your work frequently.

You can also do immense damage to a worksheet by some unintended formatting change or an incorrect formula applied to the wrong range of cells. Always save the worksheet before starting any potentially disastrous action.

Basic steps

1 Click on File in the menu bar and then on Save in the menu that drops down. A standard Windows 95 file box appears.

2 Double-click on the drive and then on the folder; do **not** store your files in the Excel 97 program folder; use a new folder for your data. (The Save As window has a button for creating a new folder if necessary.)

Select drive and folder

Click to create new folder

① ②

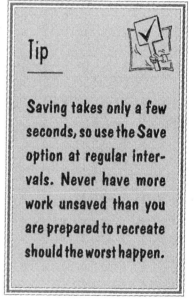

Tip

Saving takes only a few seconds, so use the Save option at regular intervals. Never have more work unsaved than you are prepared to recreate should the worst happen.

3 Type a filename, following the usual Windows 95 rules. If the file may be used on DOS systems, restrict the name to a maximum of eight numbers and letters, with no spaces. Avoid using the other permitted characters, though the dash (-) or underscore (_) can sometimes be useful. Do not enter an extension; Excel automatically adds .XLS for you.

4 Click on Save.

The file is saved, the new name appears on the title bar, and you can continue editing.

The next time you choose File | Save you will not have to supply a name; the current worksheet will replace the previous version in the file.

You will need to devise some logical naming scheme for your Excel files. Names need to be brief but remind you of what they contain. Bear in mind that you may want to create several different versions of the same file, so allow for the inclusion of some further identification (e.g. Sales 97 North Actual, Sales 97 West Projected).

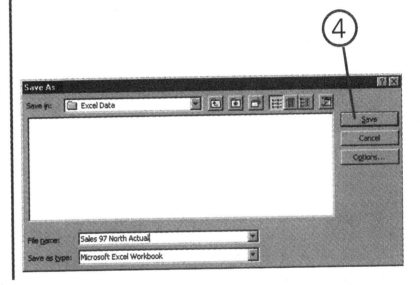

Toolbar shortcuts for File menu

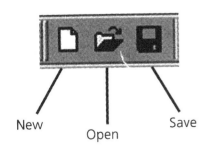

New   Save
    Open

Tip

If you need to keep copies of previous versions of a file, do so by storing them in different folders. For instance, if you update files monthly, include the month and year in the folder name.

21

You can add other information relating to the file using the File | Properties option. Enter any relevant details and click on OK. Resave the file with File | Save.

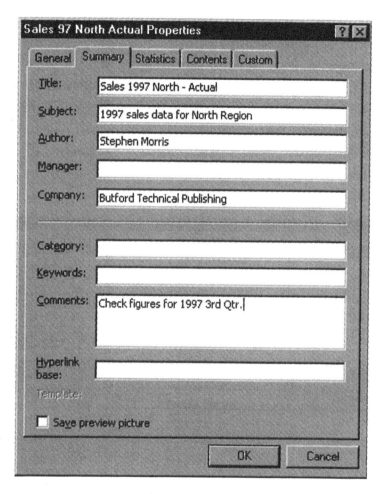

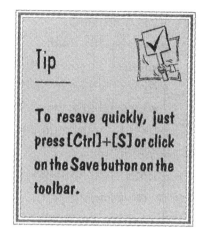

Tip

To resave quickly, just press [Ctrl]+[S] or click on the Save button on the toolbar.

If you want to save a new version of the worksheet, leaving the original intact, choose Save As from the File menu, instead of Save. You are then given the opportunity to enter a new name or choose a new folder.

When you save with a new name, the original file is unchanged. This gives you a simple way to use an existing file as the basis for a new one.

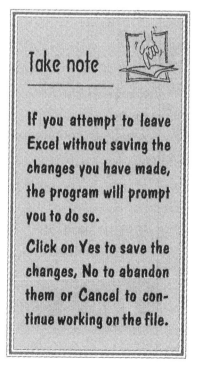

Take note

If you attempt to leave Excel without saving the changes you have made, the program will prompt you to do so.

Click on Yes to save the changes, No to abandon them or Cancel to continue working on the file.

The worksheet window

Tip

Unless it is essential that you see other windows while working on a sheet, keep the Excel 97 window maximised. Otherwise, the screen can become very confusing.

The Excel 97 display considered so far has actually consisted of two windows: the main Excel window and a subsidiary window containing the worksheet file. Initially, the subsidiary window is maximised, so it completely fills the parent window (the Excel window).

If you click on the lower of the two maximise buttons, the second window will be reduced in size and the distinction between the two will become more apparent.

This is a useful option when you need to see two sheets at once (see page 98). At other times, you will have a greater workspace if you maximise the worksheet window.

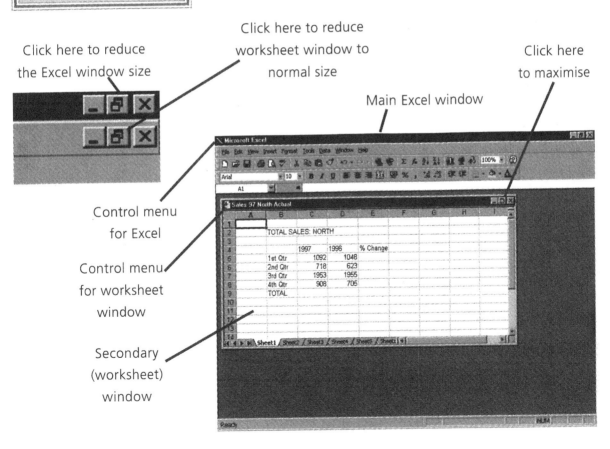

Click here to reduce the Excel window size

Click here to reduce worksheet window to normal size

Click here to maximise

Main Excel window

Control menu for Excel

Control menu for worksheet window

Secondary (worksheet) window

Closing a file

You can close the secondary window without leaving Excel. This gives you a completely empty Excel window, into which you can load a new worksheet.

When the window has been closed, most options in the drop-down menus will be greyed out, indicating that they are unavailable.

There are several ways to close the worksheet file:

- ☐ Select Close from the File menu.

- ☐ Click on the secondary window's control menu and then on Close.

- ☐ Press **[Ctrl]+[W]**.

- ☐ Click on the secondary window's close button.

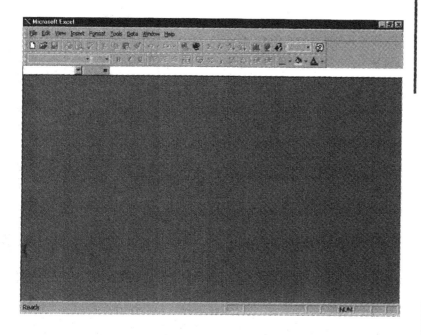

Tip

To start a new file, select File|New and then choose either the default Workbook or one of the supplied templates. Alternatively, click on the New button on the toolbar.

Take note

If you try to close the worksheet when it contains unsaved data, you are given the chance to save the file.

Loading a worksheet

There are three ways of loading an Excel worksheet:

☐ Select Open from the File menu, then choose the drive, folder and file from the file-list box.

☐ Click on the Open button on the toolbar as a shortcut to the File|Open option.

☐ Click on one of the most recently used files, which are listed at the bottom of the File menu.

Providing you have saved your worksheet, it can be easily loaded again the next time you start up Excel 97.

The File menu contains an option to load a worksheet (Open) and lists recently-used files. There is also a New option, which should be used if you want to start again from scratch.

There is no need to reload the worksheet if Excel has been temporarily suspended: just click on any visible part of the Excel window or, if it has been minimised, click on the Excel button at the bottom of the desktop. Alternatively, select Excel using **[Alt]+[Tab]** or **[Alt]+[Esc]**.

Start a new file

Re-open an existing file

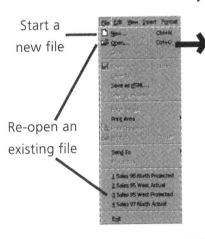

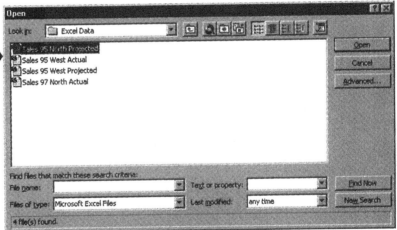

Take note

You can have more than one worksheet open at any time. If you already have a worksheet open, then loading another one does not close the first one. For details of how to handle several worksheets at once, see Section 11.

Summary of Section 3

❑ The File menu has options for saving and resaving worksheets. Files should be saved frequently (using the **[Ctrl]+[S]** shortcut keys).

❑ The Excel 97 display consists of two windows: the main Excel window and a subsidiary window. Each has its own set of buttons for minimising, maximising etc.

❑ Closing the main window also closes the worksheet window.

❑ Close the worksheet window before starting a new sheet (unless you want two sheets open at the same time).

❑ To start a new worksheet, select File I New, then click on the default Workbook or select a template from one of the folders.

❑ To load an existing sheet, select File I Open or click on the worksheet name in the File menu.

❑ The toolbar has buttons for the New, Open and Save options.

4 Formulae

Entering a formula

A **formula** is used to calculate the value of a cell from the contents of other cells. For instance, formulae may be used to calculate totals or averages, produce percentages or find the minimum and maximum values in ranges.

A formula consists of a mathematical or text **expression**, which refers to other cells or to constant values. The components of the formula are linked together by **operators** (+, – etc.)

Formulae must start with an =, + or – sign.

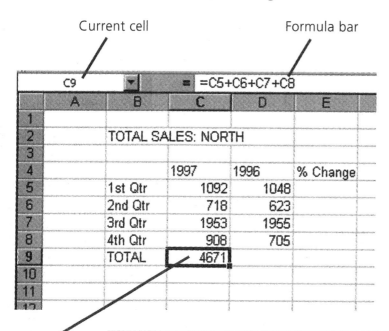

Current cell

Formula bar

Result of formula

Take note

There is an easier way of doing this type of calculation, using the SUM function — see page 40.

see page 40.

Basic steps

To enter a formula:

1 Click on the cell where you want the result of the formula to be displayed (e.g. C9).

2 Type the formula. For example:

=c5+c6+c7+c8

(You can use either upper or lower case letters for cell references.) The formula appears simultaneously in the cell and the formula bar.

3 Press **[Enter]**. The result of the calculation is shown in the cell.

When you click on this cell again, the formula is shown in the formula bar, where it can be edited. When you click on the formula bar or double-click on the cell, cell references in the formula are shown in different colours, and the cells concerned are highlighted by boxes in the same colours.

To edit a formula:

1 Click on the cell containing the formula.

2 Click on the formula in the formula bar.

3 With the usual cursor and editing keys, make the corrections.

4 Press **[Enter]**. The new result is displayed.

If you make a mistake that results in a formula which cannot be calculated (for instance, dividing by zero or referring to a text cell), Excel displays #VALUE! in the cell.

Other errors may be harder to identify and will not produce an error message. For instance, typing a – sign instead of + gives a valid answer but produces the wrong value.

Error in formula

| | | = =C5+C6+C7+B8 |
| C9 | ▼ | |

	A	B	C	D	E
1					
2		TOTAL SALES: NORTH			
3					
4			1997	1996	% Change
5		1st Qtr	1092	1048	
6		2nd Qtr	718	623	
7		3rd Qtr	1953	1955	
8		4th Qtr	908	705	
9		TOTAL	#VALUE!		
10					
11					

Error indicator

29

Calculation options

Excel recalculates the worksheet whenever you make a change to any item of data. The program adopts an intelligent approach; only those formulae that are affected by the change are recalculated, and the calculations are done in a logical order. The formulae that refer to the changed cell are recalculated first; if this results in changes to other cells, then any further formulae that are affected are also calculated, and so on.

This seems impressive when you first use a spreadsheet program but can become tedious, particularly for large, complicated worksheets, where a full recalculation may take some time. In such cases, you can use the Options item in the Tools menu to switch automatic calculation off. Click on the Calculation tab and a range of options is available; clicking on Manual means that in future you will have to press **[F9]** to force a recalculation.

The Calculation tab from the Tools | Options menu gives you these alternatives:

☐ **Automatic** recalculates affected cells in a logical order – the default.

☐ **Automatic Except Tables** recalculates everything except data tables.

☐ **Manual** recalculates the sheet only when you press **[F9]**.

Leave **Recalculate Before Save** switched on – this forces a recalculation in Manual mode whenever you save the file.

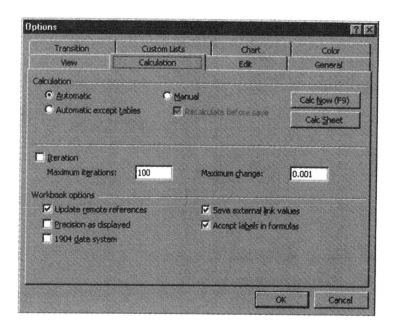

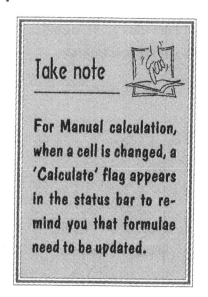

Take note

For Manual calculation, when a cell is changed, a 'Calculate' flag appears in the status bar to remind you that formulae need to be updated.

Operators

The following numeric operators are recognised:

^   Raising to the power (e.g. 2^3 is 2^3)

*   Multiplication

/   Division

+   Addition

–   Subtraction

You can also use:

–   Negation (in front of a number)

%   Percentage (after a number)

For text formulae:

&   Combines strings (concatenation)

Five main arithmetic operators are used to determine how values are combined. A formula consists of an alternating sequence of values and operators, usually starting and ending with a value (the only exceptions are the use of a minus sign to negate a value and the percentage symbol).

The calculation is not carried out from left to right but according to the following rules:

- Raising to the power (^) is done first (also called **exponentiation**).

- Next come any multiplications and divisions (* /).

- Finally, additions and subtractions (+ –) are performed.

For text calculations, only the & operator is allowed. This adds one string to the end of another. You cannot use + to add strings in a formula.

Take note

Plus and minus signs may also appear in formulae as part of numbers in Scientific format – see page 62.

Take note

You can precede a value with a minus sign (–) to negate it or follow a value with a percentage sign (%). For example, 2*–3 gives –6, multiplying by 5% is the same as multiplying by 0.05. Negations and percentages are done before any of the other operations.

Using brackets

You can use brackets (parentheses) to change the order of calculation. Anything inside a pair of brackets is calculated first.

For example, the percentage change in E5 is calculated by:

=(C5–D5)/D5

The brackets are essential here; if there were no brackets the division would be carried out first, giving a result of C5 – 1.

Main points

- ☐ Calculations start inside the innermost pair of brackets and work outwards.

- ☐ Every opening bracket must have a corresponding closing bracket (Excel highlights the matching opening bracket for you every time you type a closing bracket).

- ☐ You can nest up to seven pairs of brackets (see opposite).

E5	▼	=	=(C5-D5)/D5	
	A	B	C	D	E
1					
2		TOTAL SALES: NORTH			
3					
4			1997	1996	% Change
5		1st Qtr	1092	1048	0.041985
6		2nd Qtr	718	623	
7		3rd Qtr	1953	1955	
8		4th Qtr	908	705	
9		TOTAL	4671		
10					
11					
12					

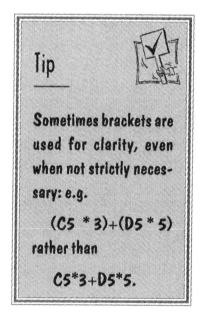

Tip

Sometimes brackets are used for clarity, even when not strictly necessary: e.g.

(C5 * 3)+(D5 * 5)

rather than

C5*3+D5*5.

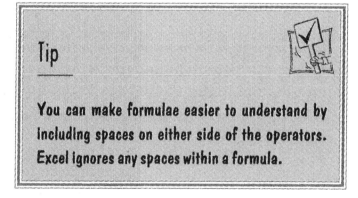

Tip

You can make formulae easier to understand by including spaces on either side of the operators. Excel ignores any spaces within a formula.

Tip

Do not use brackets to indicate negative numbers
in a formula; use the −
sign instead. Only use
round brackets () in for-
mulae; square brackets []
and curly brackets { } will
not be accepted.

You can also **nest** brackets: i.e. place one set of brackets inside another.

For example:

$$=((100-(A8+1)*5)+0.5)/10$$

If the value of A8 is 7, the formula is calculated as follows:

$$((100-(7+1)*5)+0.5)/10$$

$$= ((100-8*5)+0.5)/10$$

$$= ((100-40)+0.5)/10$$

$$= (60+0.5)/10$$

$$= 60.5/10$$

$$= 6.05$$

Don't let your formulae get too complicated. It is better to split a complex formula over several cells than to build them all into a single formula. This allows you to find errors more easily and to check intermediate values. For example:

In D5:	= A8 + 1
In D6:	= 100 − (D5 * 5)
In D7:	= (D6 + 0.5) / 10

Tip

You can put any intermediate formula in a row or column that is then hidden — see page 88.

Ranges

Many operations within Excel require you to mark out **ranges** of cells. For example, you may want to add together all the numbers in a range of cells; you will also want to change the display format for ranges of cells (see Section 7).

A range is a group of cells that form a rectangle and it is identified by the cells in the top left-hand and bottom right-hand corners of the rectangle, separated by a colon. For instance, the range reference A1:B3 identifies a range containing six cells: A1, A2, A3, B1, B2, B3.

A range can be anything from a single cell to the entire worksheet.

To mark a range on the worksheet:

1 Move the pointer to the cell in the top left-hand corner of the range.

2 Press and hold the mouse button, then drag the pointer to the cell at the bottom right-hand corner of the range.

3 Release the mouse button; the range is highlighted.

Alternatively, click on the first cell, press and hold **[Shift]**, then click on the last cell.

	A	B	C	D	E	F	G
1							
2							
3		B3:B3			D3:F3		
4							
5							
6		B5:B8			D5:F8		
7							
8							
9							
10							
11							

Start dragging here

Finish dragging here

	A	B	C	D	E	F
1						
2		TOTAL SALES: NORTH				
3						
4			1997	1996	% Change	
5		1st Qtr	1092	1048	0.041985	
6		2nd Qtr	718	623		
7		3rd Qtr	1953	1955		
8		4th Qtr	908	705		
9		TOTAL	4671			
10						
11						

Options

- To mark a single cell just click on it.

- To mark a whole row or column, click on the row number or column letter.

- To mark the entire worksheet, click on the square in the top left-hand corner of the worksheet.

You can highlight whole rows or columns, or the entire sheet by clicking on the worksheet borders.

You can select more than one range at a time by holding down the **[Ctrl]** key while you mark the blocks, rows or columns.

If you click anywhere else after you have marked a block, the block marking disappears.

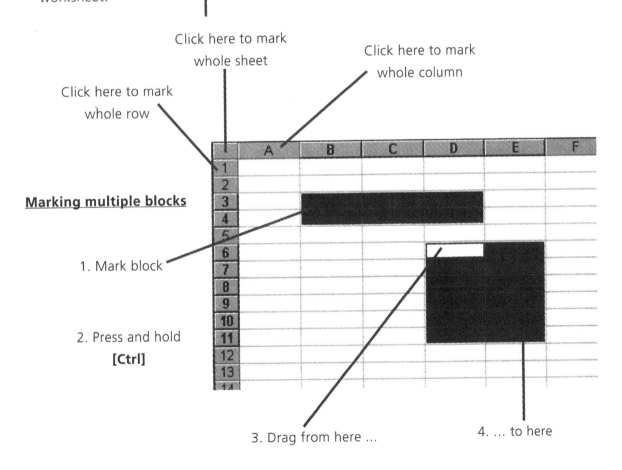

Click here to mark whole sheet

Click here to mark whole column

Click here to mark whole row

Marking multiple blocks

1. Mark block

2. Press and hold **[Ctrl]**

3. Drag from here ...

4. ... to here

Names

Working with ranges can be cumbersome, particularly on large worksheets where a formula may refer to a range that is some distance away. So Excel allows you to attach a name to any cell or range. This name can be used in any formula in place of the cell or range reference.

Names can be up to 255 characters (far more than you should ever use), consisting of letters, numbers, full stops and underscore characters. Other characters are not allowed. The name should start with a letter.

Upper and lower case letters are treated the same but the name is stored exactly as you type it, so it is a good idea to mix lower case letters and capitals. When a name is referenced in a formula, Excel converts it to the same mixture of upper and lower case.

Cell to be named

Suggested name

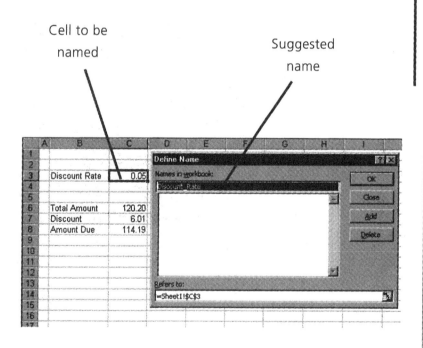

Basic steps

To add a name:

1 Mark the cell or range to which the name is to be applied.

2 Select the Name option from the Insert menu.

3 Click on Define in the sub-menu.

4 Type the name and press **[Enter]**.

The names that you create can be listed in the name box in the toolbar (where the cell reference is usually shown). Click on the arrow on the right of the box to see the list drop down.

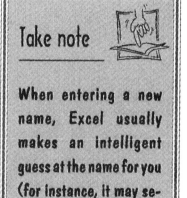

Take note

When entering a new name, Excel usually makes an intelligent guess at the name for you (for instance, it may select an adjacent label, replacing any spaces with underscore characters).

To use existing labels as names:

1 Mark a range consisting of the labels and the cells to which they are to be attached.

2 Select Insert I Name I Create.

3 Identify the location of the names. For example, **Left Column** means that the names are in a column to the left of the data range.

4 Press **[Enter]**.

Click to select name

To use a name in a formula, simply substitute the name for the cell reference. In the example in the illustration, the formulae for Discount and Amount Due were originally:

$$= \text{C6*C3}$$

$$= \text{C6–C7}$$

These can be changed to:

$$= \textbf{Total\_Amount*Discount\_Rate}$$

$$= \textbf{Total\_Amount–Discount}$$

Names can either be typed in full or inserted by clicking on the data cell as you are entering the formula.

Amount_Due		=	=Total_Amount-Discount		
Amount_Due		C	D	E	
Discount					
Discount_Rate					
Total_Amount					
3	Discount Rate	0.05			
4					
5					
6	Total Amount	120.20			
7	Discount	6.01			
8	Amount Due	114.19			

Total Amount	120.20
Discount	6.01
Amount Due	114.19

Create Names ? X

Create names in
- [ ] Top row
- [x] Left column
- [ ] Bottom row
- [ ] Right column

OK   Cancel

Tip

Names are particularly useful where a range is referenced more than once on the worksheet. If you change the definition of the name so that it refers to another range, you will not have to change any of the formulae that use that name.

Summary of Section 4

❑   Formulae are used for calculating cell values from the contents of other cells.

❑   Formulae start with an =, + or – sign, which is followed by an **expression**.

❑   Formulae are usually updated automatically every time a change is made to the data; alternatively, you can select Manual calculation mode, when calculations are only done if you press **[F9]** or the sheet is saved.

❑   Raising to the power (^) is always done first, followed by multiplication (*) and division (/), and finally addition (+) and subtraction (-).

❑   Values can be negated by putting a minus sign in front of them, or converted to percentages.

❑   Text entries can be combined with the & operator.

❑   Brackets change the order of calculation; the innermost expression is calculated first.

❑   Some operations require a **range** of cells, which is a rectangular block defined by the top-left and bottom-right cells, separated by a colon (e.g. A1:B8).

❑   Names can be defined for cells and ranges, and these may be used in formulae.

5 Functions

The SUM function

Using SUM

Excel contains a large number of built-in **functions**. These are special routines that can be used within a formula to perform particular tasks. For example, the most commonly used function is SUM, which calculates the total of all the cells in a specified range. Other arithmetic functions include AVERAGE to calculate the average of a range, and MIN and MAX to find the smallest and largest numbers in a range, plus many others.

The function name is followed by a pair of brackets containing one or more **arguments**. If there is more than one argument, these are separated by commas. In the case of SUM, there need be only one argument: the range to be totalled.

Functions are used in a formula in the same way as a constant value or cell reference. When the formula is calculated, the function returns a value which replaces it in the formula.

The SUM function can be used in the Sales 97 worksheet to replace the rather clumsy formula in C9.

1 Click on C9.

2 Start typing to replace the existing entry:

   =sum(

3 Drag the mouse pointer over the range C5:C8. As you do so the range appears in the formula.

4 Type the closing bracket and press **[Enter]**.

Take note

The SUM function can take more than one argument. For example, SUM(B6,C9:D12) returns the total of the number in cell B6 plus all the numbers in the range C9:C12.

Tip

Although you can type the range directly into the function, marking it by dragging gives you a better chance of getting it right.

To use the AutoSum button:

1 Click on the cell where the total is required.

2 Click on the AutoSum button. Excel suggests the range to be totalled and marks it with a flashing outline. Check the range very carefully.

3 If the wrong range has been suggested, select a new one by dragging the pointer over it.

4 Press **[Enter]**.

The SUM function has its own **AutoSum** button on the toolbar. This button lets you apply a SUM function with as few as three keypresses/button clicks. However, it requires some care; it is just as easy to get the sum wrong!

IF		▼	X ✓ =	=SUM(C5:C8)	
	A	B	C	D	E
1					
2		TOTAL SALES: NORTH			
3					
4			1997	1996	% Change
5		1st Qtr	1092	1048	0.041985
6		2nd Qtr	718	623	
7		3rd Qtr	1953	1955	
8		4th Qtr	908	705	
9		TOTAL	=SUM(C5:C8)		
10					

Take note

AutoSum suggests the column of numbers above the current cell or the row to the left. If there are numbers both above and to the left, the block above is chosen. Any blank cells immediately above or to the left of the current cell are included in the block but if there are gaps in the numbers above or to the left, only those up to the gap are marked.

AutoSum

Other functions

Excel comes equipped with a huge variety of built-in functions – over 200 in all. These fall into a number of categories:

- The **maths & trigonometry** functions include SUM and some more exotic variations (e.g. SUMSQ to calculate the sum of the squares of the values). All the most commonly-used trigonometric functions are available (such as sine, cosine, tangent), including functions to convert between radians and degrees.

- The **statistical** functions range from the simple AVERAGE function to a function for the chi-squared distribution (CHIDIST).

- The **financial** functions perform a comprehensive set of accountancy tasks. For example, DDB uses the double-declining balance method for calculating depreciation; NPV calculates the net present value of an amount that has been invested.

Help for functions

To use any function:

1 Type the formula up to the point where the function is required.

2 Type the function name and an opening bracket.

3 Mark the first argument (a cell or range).

4 If there is a second argument, type a comma (,).

5 Type further arguments and commas as required.

6 Following the last argument, type a closing bracket and press **[Enter]**.

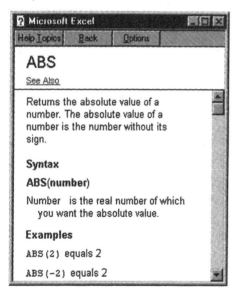

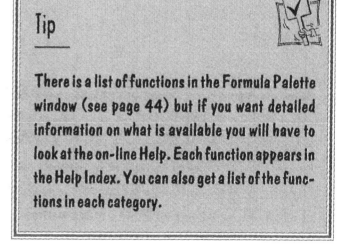

Tip

There is a list of functions in the Formula Palette window (see page 44) but if you want detailed information on what is available you will have to look at the on-line Help. Each function appears in the Help Index. You can also get a list of the functions in each category.

- The **date & time** functions perform tasks such as extracting the month from a cell containing a date (MONTH) or returning the current date and time (NOW).

- The **text** functions let you work with text entries in cells; for example, LEN returns the length of an item of text, LEFT returns a string of characters from the left-hand side of some text and FIND scans a cell for a particular character or string.

- The **lookup & reference** functions are applied to lists and tables; the **database** functions perform limited operations on database records.

- The **logical** functions apply logical AND, OR and NOT operations, returning results of TRUE or FALSE. Most importantly, they include the IF function for conditional calculations.

- The **information** functions relate to Excel itself. For instance, CELL returns information about a specified cell, ISERROR tells you whether or not a cell contains an error (e.g. #VALUE!).

	A	B	C	D
1				
2				
3		Text Functions		
4				
5		LEN(b3)		14
6		LEFT(b3, 4)	Text	
7		RIGHT(b3, 9)	Functions	
8		MID(b3, 11, 3)	ion	
9		FIND("Fun", b3)		6
10				

43

The Formula Palette

There are many different functions in Excel and by far the easiest way of using them is through the Formula Palette. This provides a dialogue box in which the functions are listed. When you click on a function, its purpose is shown at the bottom of the box.

The Formula Palette also provides a dialogue box for entering the value for each argument, so you can be certain that you are supplying the correct number of arguments and that they are in the right order.

Each entry can be a constant value, or an expression. You can even **nest** another function by clicking on the small Formula Palette buttons (marked **fx**). Functions can be nested up to seven levels.

To use the Formula Palette:

1 Type the formula up to the point where you need a function.

2 Click on the Formula Palette button, marked with **fx**.

3 Select the Function Category to reduce the list of functions and click on the required Function Name. (Click on the **All** category if you don't know which set the required function is in.)

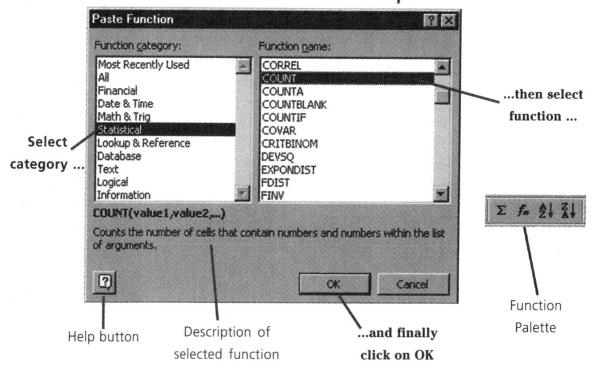

Select category ...

...then select function ...

Help button

Description of selected function

...and finally click on OK

Function Palette

4 Click OK to bring up the
main palette, where the
arguments can be
entered.

5 Click on OK and the
function will be added to
the formula.

6 Click on the formula bar
to add more elements.

Click to hide
palette while
marking cells

Click to
change
function

Enter
arguments

Values in
range

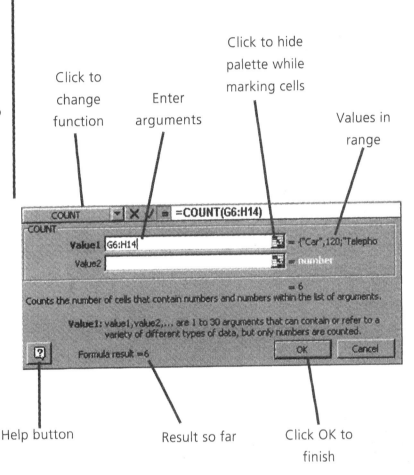

Help button

Result so far

Click OK to
finish

General error message for formulae

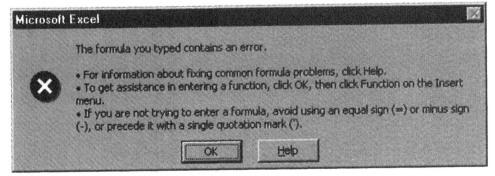

The IF function

One of the most usefulExcel's many functions is the IF function. This **conditional function** returns two possible values, depending on the result of some comparison.

The function has three arguments:

- The comparison to be performed (e.g. **C5<90** compares the value of cell C5 to see if it is less than 90)

- The value to be returned if the result of the comparison is true

- The value to be returned if the result of the comparison is false

The two return values may be constant values, text or further expressions.

Operators

The following operators can be used in a comparison:

<	Less than
<=	Less than or equal
>	Greater than
>=	Greater than or equal
=	Equal
<>	Not equal

The IF function is included in the Logical category.

Current values

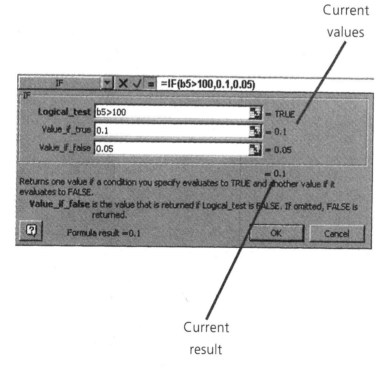

Current result

Tip

Don't make IF statements too complex; it is better to use a series of related functions where the result in one cell is passed to the next function in another cell. Otherwise, finding errors becomes very difficult.

Comparison expressions can be combined with the following logical operators:

AND   True if both expressions are true

OR   True if either or both expressions are true

You can also use the NOT operator, which reverses the result.

For example, in the first illustration below, the Discount % column has a value of 0.10 if the Quantity is greater than 100, or 0.05 otherwise. The formula in E5 is:

=IF(B5>100,0.1,0.05)

This formula is copied over the range E6:E8. (See Section 6 for instructions on how to copy a formula.)

Complex decisions can be made by **nesting** IF functions. For instance, the discount calculation in the second illustration contains the formula in E8:

=IF(Discount_Rate=0,0,IF(Discount_Rate=1,0.1,0.05))

If the cell named **Discount_Rate** has a value of 0, the value returned is 0; otherwise, a further test is carried out, with a rate of 1 returning 0.1 and anything else giving 0.05.

You can also use the IF function to return warning messages if an input value is outside a permitted range.

	A	B	C	D	E	F	G
1							
2							
3		Quantity	Unit Price	Sub-total	Discount %	Discount	Total
4							
5		120	2.32	278.40	0.10	27.84	250.56
6		86	3.45	296.70	0.05	14.84	281.87
7		100	1.28	128.00	0.05	6.40	121.60
8		200	0.95	190.00	0.10	19.00	171.00
9							

	A	B	C	D	E	F	G
1							
2							
3			Discount Rate	1	(Enter 0, 1 or 2)		
4							
5							
6		Quantity	Unit Price	Sub-total	Discount %	Discount	Total
7							
8		120	2.32	278.40	0.10	27.84	250.56
9		86	3.45	296.70	0.10	29.67	267.03
10		100	1.28	128.00	0.10	12.80	115.20
11		200	0.95	190.00	0.10	19.00	171.00
12							

Summary of Section 5

□ A **function** is a built-in routine for performing some special action. For instance, SUM totals the values in a range.

□ Functions consist of a keyword and a pair of brackets. The brackets contain one or more **arguments**, separated by commas. Some special functions have no arguments (e.g. NOW to return the current date and time).

□ A **SUM** formula can be inserted using the AutoSum button on the toolbar.

□ There are over 200 functions, in nine main categories. There are also 40 engineering functions, which may be added by running Excel Setup.

□ The **Formula Palette** provides an easy way to add a function to a formula, allowing you to choose the function and then fill in the arguments.

□ The **IF** function returns two alternative values, depending on whether the result of some logical test is true or false.

6 Formula operations

Copying formulae

In most worksheets, you will need to repeat the same formula in a number of cells or fill a range of cells with a similar formula. Excel makes it very easy for you to copy a formula to other cells.

For example, the formula in C9 is **=SUM(C5:C8)** and this can be copied to D9. Excel does not make an exact duplicate of the formula; it assumes that the copied formula will refer to cells in the same relative position. That is, it sees the formula in C9 as an instruction to add together the contents of the four cells above. When the formula is copied, the result is still the same; the new formula adds together the cells above, becoming SUM(D5:D8).

To copy a single formula:

1 Click on the cell to be copied, so that it is highlighted.

2 Press **[Ctrl]+[C]** to copy the formula to the Windows clipboard (or select Edit | Copy).

3 Click on the cell where the copy is to appear, or drag the pointer to highlight a range of cells.

4 Press **[Enter]** (or select Edit | Paste) and the formula will be repeated in each of the highlighted cells.

	1997	1996	% Change
1st Qtr	1092	1048	0.041985
2nd Qtr	718	623	
3rd Qtr	1953	1955	
4th Qtr	908	705	
TOTAL	4671		

① ③

Take note

The same process can be used for cells that contain constant values or text strings; the values will be repeated in all the marked cells.

To copy a range of cells:

1 Mark the range to be copied.

2 Press **[Ctrl]+[C]** to copy all the formulae to the clipboard.

3 Click on the cell that will be in the top left-hand corner when the range is copied.

4 Press **[Enter]** to complete the copy.

The % Change formula in E5 can be copied down the column by clicking on E5, pressing **[Ctrl]+[C]**, dragging over the range E6:E9 and pressing **[Enter]**.

Click and press
[Ctrl]+[C]

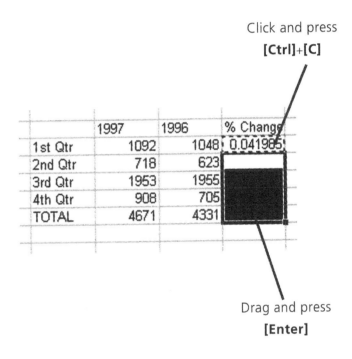

	1997	1996	% Change
1st Qtr	1092	1048	0.041985
2nd Qtr	718	623	
3rd Qtr	1953	1955	
4th Qtr	908	705	
TOTAL	4671	4331	

Drag and press
[Enter]

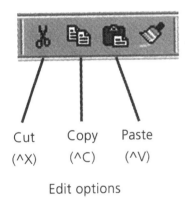

Cut   Copy   Paste
(^X)   (^C)   (^V)

Edit options

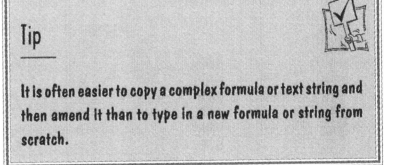

Tip

It is often easier to copy a complex formula or text string and then amend it than to type in a new formula or string from scratch.

Relative and absolute references

When you copy a formula to another cell, any cell references are automatically updated so that they refer to the cell in the same relative position; these are called **relative cell references**.

Often, you want the formula to refer to the **same** cell, regardless of where the formula is copied. For instance, an invoice may take the discount rate from a single cell. To do this, each part of the cell reference is preceded by a $ sign; for example, a formula that refers to $C$24 will always use the value in C24, no matter where it is copied to. This is an **absolute cell reference**.

Sometimes you need to keep one part of the reference absolute while allowing the other part to change. For instance, the items in a table may be based on the values at the top of each column or on the left of each row. In these cases, the $ sign is placed in front of the part that is to remain unchanged. These are **mixed cell references**.

Options

Suppose that a formula in C54 referring to C24 is copied over the range C54:D56. There are four possible combinations for the reference in the new formulae:

☐ For a relative reference, both parts are changed when the formula is copied (e.g. C24 becomes C25, C26, D24, D25, D26).

☐ For an absolute reference, nothing changes (e.g. $C$24 stays as $C$24 no matter where it is copied).

☐ If the column is fixed, only the row number changes (e.g. $C24 becomes $C25, $C26, $C24, $C25, $C26).

☐ If the row is fixed, only the column letter changes (e.g. C$24 becomes C$24, C$24, D$24, D$24, D$24).

Formula in C6 uses three types of reference

C6	▼	= $B6 * (1-C$5) * (1+$E$2)		
	A	B	C	D	E
1					
2		**Gross Price Table**		VAT Rate:	10.00%
3					
4				Discount	
5			**5%**	**10%**	**20%**
6		**1.00**	1.05	0.99	0.88
7	Net	**2.00**	2.09	1.98	1.76
8	Price	**3.00**	3.14	2.97	2.64
9		**4.00**	4.18	3.96	3.52
10		**5.00**	5.23	4.95	4.40
11		**6.00**	6.27	5.94	5.28
12					

Moving cells and ranges

To move the contents of a cell or range:

1 Click on the cell or drag over the range.

2 Press **[Ctrl]+[X]** to cut the highlighted area to the clipboard (the cells are cleared).

3 Click on the cell that is to be the top left-hand corner of the range.

4 Press **[Enter]**. The contents of the cell or range appear in their new position.

As an alternative to copying the contents of cells (so that you have multiple copies), you can **move** the contents to a new location (clearing out the originals).

The principles are similar to those for copying but you will end up with a single copy of the original range in a new position.

Tip

When a formula is moved, the cell references are not updated (unlike the result when a formula is copied). If you want the references changed, you should copy the formula and then delete the original.

Drag and press
[Ctrl]+[X]

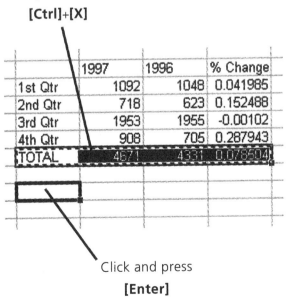

	1997	1996	% Change
1st Qtr	1092	1048	0.041985
2nd Qtr	718	623	0.152488
3rd Qtr	1953	1955	-0.00102
4th Qtr	908	705	0.287943
TOTAL	4671	4331	0.078504

Click and press
[Enter]

Take note

You can transpose data (change rows to columns and vice versa) using the TRANSPOSE function. For instructions on how to do this, activate the Office Assistant and type 'transpose' in the query box.

Summary of Section 6

- ❑ A formula can be copied to another cell, or copied over a range of cells. A range of cells can be copied to another location.

- ❑ Unless you specify otherwise, all cell references are updated so that they refer to the cells in the same **relative** positions.

- ❑ Cell references can be made **absolute** by putting $ in front of each part (e.g. $B$25 always refers to cell B25).

- ❑ Mixed cell references keep one part fixed while the other varies (e.g. $B25 always refers to column B but the row number may change; B$25 always refers to row 25 but the column may change).

- ❑ Cells and ranges can also be moved; the cell references in formulae are not updated after the move.

7 Number formats

Applying number formats

Up until this point, numeric values have been displayed with the format that best suits them in each individual case: as whole numbers or with a limited number of decimal places or using scientific format. This is the **General** format and you will usually want to change it in different parts of the worksheet. For example, monetary values will usually be displayed with exactly two decimal places, or you may want to round the results of calculations to the nearest whole number or a specific number of decimal places.

The format for a cell or range is altered using the Format | Cells command.

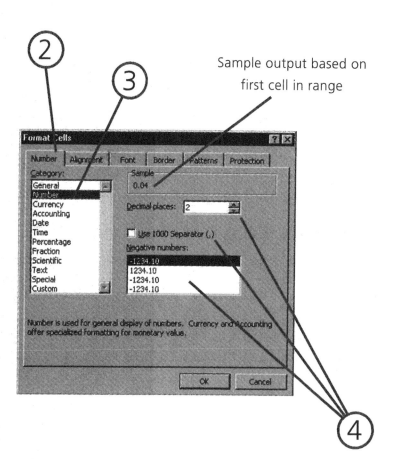

Sample output based on first cell in range

Basic steps

1   Click on the cell to be formatted or mark a range of cells.

2   Select Cells from the Format menu, then click on the Number tab.

3   Choose the category that applies to the type of data being formatted.

4   Select the precise format, depending on category (e.g. for the Number category, select the number of decimal places, whether or not to use a thousands separator, and how to handle negative numbers).

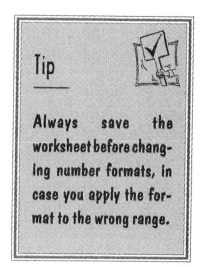

Tip

Always save the worksheet before changing number formats, in case you apply the format to the wrong range.

Format options

Number formats include integers (whole numbers) and various levels of decimal places.

Currency formats are similar to Number formats but insert a currency symbol at the front of the displayed number.

Date and **Time** formats provide several alternatives for the display of date and time values (see Section 8).

Percentage formats convert all values to percentages.

Fraction formats allow you to display fractions (e.g. $^{40}/_{47}$ rather than 0.851).

Scientific formats use the exponential style.

Accounting formats are similar to Number formats but use a dash to represent zero values.

Special formats are not applicable to the UK.

When you choose a number format, the Sample line in the dialogue box shows you what the first highlighted cell will look like when it is displayed.

There is a wide range of possible formats built into the system. Some of these are described in more detail in the rest of this section.

Percentage format with 2 decimal places

TOTAL SALES: NORTH			
	1997	1996	% Change
1st Qtr	1092	1048	4.20%
2nd Qtr	718	623	15.25%
3rd Qtr	1953	1955	-0.10%
4th Qtr	908	705	28.79%
TOTAL	4671	4331	7.85%

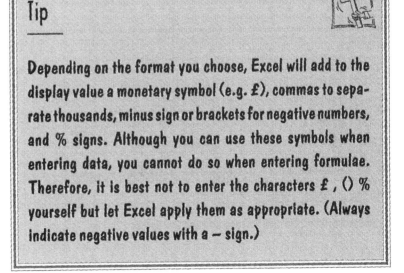

Tip

Depending on the format you choose, Excel will add to the display value a monetary symbol (e.g. £), commas to separate thousands, minus sign or brackets for negative numbers, and % signs. Although you can use these symbols when entering data, you cannot do so when entering formulae. Therefore, it is best not to enter the characters £ , () % yourself but let Excel apply them as appropriate. (Always indicate negative values with a – sign.)

Decimal places

In most cases you will want to restrict the number of decimal places used in displayed values. The various formats on offer limit the number of figures after the decimal point. The Custom format gives you complete control over the display style (see page 68). (Note that values are stored with 15 significant figures, which includes all figures before and after the decimal point.)

(see page 68)

Tip

Do not use more decimal places than are reasonable or necessary. For instance, with monetary values there is rarely a need for more than two decimal places.

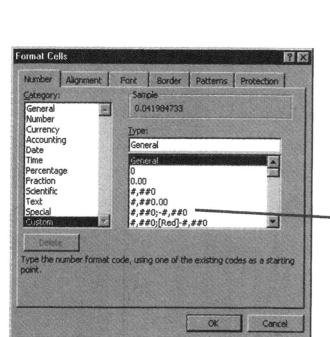

The format codes give an idea of how numbers will be displayed: see page 68 for details

see page 68 for details

Take note

A zero (0) in the format notation indicates that a digit will always be displayed, even if it is a zero; # indicates that leading and trailing zeros will be ignored.

Take note

The General format displays up to nine decimal places.

Several categories supply values with a number of decimal places:

- The **integer** format (the **Number** category with **0** decimal places) displays values as whole numbers.

- The various **floating point** formats (also in the **Number** category) give an exact number of decimal places; if necessary, extra 0s are added at the end to pad out the number.

- The **Percentage** format can be a bit confusing; formatting 0.175 as a percentage results in a display of **17.5%**.

- The **Currency** format works like a floating point value but inserts a currency symbol (e.g. £).

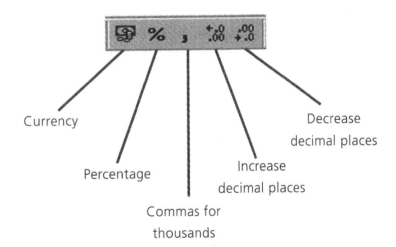

Currency

Percentage

Commas for thousands

Increase decimal places

Decrease decimal places

Stored and displayed values

When the General format is applied, the displayed value will have as many decimal places as are necessary for the value on screen to match that stored in memory (providing the column is wide enough). The value in any cell, whether entered directly or calculated from a formula, is stored in memory with 15 significant figures.

However, as soon as a different format is applied, with the number of decimal places limited, the value will be rounded for the display. For example, with an integer display format, any value ending in .5 or more will be rounded **up** to the next whole number while those less than .5 are rounded **down**. Thus 3.5, 3.501 and 3.95 are all rounded up to 4 but 3.01, 3.45 and 3.49995 are all rounded down to 3.

The most important point is that all calculations use the **stored** value, rather than the **displayed** value. This can lead to some surprising results, even when there is no division involved.

	Actual value	Integer display	
A	2.45	2	
B	2.35	2	
C = A + B	4.8	5	2 + 2 = 5 !
D = C * 3	14.4	14	5 * 3 = 14 !

Precision as displayed

Sometimes you want the stored value to match the displayed value: for example, most calculations involving money will need the result stored to the nearest penny and not with a dozen decimal places!

The Tools | Options | Calculation | Precision As Displayed option permanently changes stored values so that they match the displayed amounts.

Take note

Precision As Displayed applies to all cells in the current file, so should be used with care. In complex calculations, rounding errors can accumulate rapidly.

The Currency format

Take note

The Regional Settings also determine features such as the date and time display formats.

When you mark a part of the worksheet with the Currency format you may find that the values are displayed with $ at the front rather than £. In this case, Windows 95 is not set up for UK use; the currency symbol is a function of Windows 95, rather than Excel 97.

To change the symbol, double-click on the Regional Settings icon in the Windows 95 Control Panel (selected from the Settings group in the Start menu). Then click on the Currency tab, enter the £ sign as the Currency Symbol and click on OK. As soon as you get back to Excel, the display will be updated.

Tip

If you need to use a different currency symbol for a particular worksheet or set of figures, do not change the Regional Settings symbol; this has a global effect which will change all currency amounts in all worksheets (as well as currencies in other Windows 95 programs). Instead, set up a custom format — see page 68.

Type symbol here

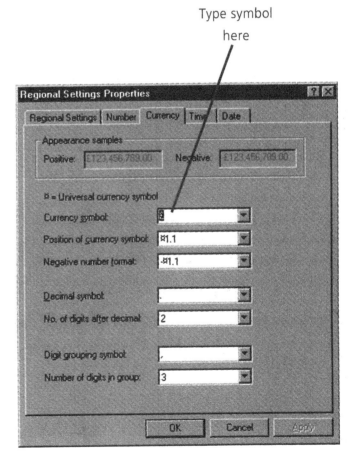

Scientific format

The **Scientific** format is used for very large and very small numbers, where the scale of the number makes it difficult to comprehend if written as a normal decimal. This format, which is most commonly found in scientific applications, is also referred to as the **exponential** format.

The format represents numbers in the form:

x.xxE±yy

The first part (x.xx) is a number in the range 1.00 to 9.99. The last part (yy) is a power of ten by which the number must be multiplied to get the required value; this is the **exponent**. For example:

$$52.3 = 5.23 \times 10 = 5.23E+01$$

$$523 = 5.23 \times 10^2 = 5.23E+02$$

$$5230 = 5.23 \times 10^3 = 5.23E+03$$

There is a special case when the number is already in the range 1 to 9.99:

$$5.23 = 5.23 \times 10^0 = 5.23E+00$$

Take note

If you enter a value in Scientific form, Excel uses that format for the cell, even if the value is not particularly large or small. For example, if you enter '5.2e1' it is displayed as '5.20E+01' and '523e34' appears as '5.23E+36'.

Effects

☐ Multiplying a number by 10 increases the exponent by 1; dividing by 10 reduces the exponent by 1.

e.g. $6.98E+04 \times 10 = 6.98E+05$

$6.98E+04 / 10 = 6.98E+03$

☐ When two numbers are multiplied together the parts on the left are multiplied and the exponents are added.

e.g. $2E+02 \times 3E+05 = 6E+07$

☐ When one number is divided by another, the division is carried out on the numbers on the left and the second exponent is subtracted from the first.

e.g. $8E+03 / 2E+02 = 4E+01$

The exponent can also be negative, indicating that the value is to be divided by 10 to a given power. For example:

$$0.523 = 5.23 / 10 = 5.23\text{E}{-}01$$

$$0.0523 = 5.23 / 10^2 = 5.23\text{E}{-}02$$

Don't get confused by this minus sign; these values are positive. A **value** is only negative if there is a minus sign on the left of the main number. For example:

$$-523 = -5.23 \times 10^2 = -5.23\text{E}{+}02$$

$$-0.0523 = -5.23 \times 10^{-2} = -5.23\text{E}{-}02$$

	A	B	C	D	E
1					
2			General	Decimal	Scientific
3		5.23 * 100000	523000	523000.00	5.23E+05
4		5.23 * 100	523	523.00	5.23E+02
5		5.23 * 10	52.3	52.30	5.23E+01
6		5.23	5.23	5.23	5.23E+00
7		5.23 /10	0.523	0.52	5.23E-01
8		5.23 /100	0.0523	0.05	5.23E-02
9		5.23 / 1000000	0.00000523	0.00	5.23E-06
10					
11		-5.23 * 100000	-523000	-523000.00	-5.23E+05
12		-5.23 * 100	-523	-523.00	-5.23E+02
13		-5.23 * 10	-52.3	-52.30	-5.23E+01
14		-5.23	-5.23	-5.23	-5.23E+00
15		-5.23 /10	-0.523	-0.52	-5.23E-01
16		-5.23 /100	-0.0523	-0.05	-5.23E-02
17		-5.23 / 1000000	-0.00000523	0.00	-5.23E-06
18					

Summary of Section 7

- ❑ By default, all cells are formatted with the General format, which applies the most suitable display style in each case.

- ❑ The format for a cell or range is changed with the Format |Cells command.

- ❑ Numbers are stored with 15 significant figures of accuracy; there are bound to be slight inaccuracies in results, particularly when divisions occur; these will not usually be a problem.

- ❑ Calculations use the stored values, not the displayed values. The stored values can be changed to match the displayed values with Tools | Options | Calculation | Precision As Displayed (which applies to the whole file).

- ❑ Formats with a fixed number of decimal places include Integer, Floating Point, Percentage, Currency and Accountancy.

- ❑ The Scientific format is normally used for very large and very small numbers.

8 Other formats

Dates and times

Excel can handle dates and times in calculations. It does this by storing any date or time as a numeric code, rather than as text.

Dates are stored as integers, representing the number of days from 31st December 1899. For example, 35065 represents 1st January 1996.

If you enter a date in the General format, Excel displays it in the form dd/mm/yy. If this is then copied to another cell, formatted as integer, the number that represents that date will be shown. Similarly, an integer formatted as a date will show in date format provided it is within the permissible range.

	A	B	C	D	E
1					
2		Date	07/05/90		
3		Date value	33000		=C2, formatted as a number
4					
5		Time	4:00 AM		
6		Time value	0.17		=C5, formatted as a number
7					
8		Value	37025.96		
9		Date & Time	14/05/2001 23:02		=C8, formatted as dd/mm/yyyy hh:mm
10					
11					

Limits

☐ The earliest date you can use is 01/03/1900, represented by the value 61.

☐ The latest date recognised by Excel is 31/12/9999, represented by 2,958,465.

Take note

The values for dates before March 1900 are incorrect, as Excel incorrectly treats 1900 as a leap year.

Tip

A date that has been entered as text can be converted to its numeric value with the DATEVALUE function. The DAY, MONTH and YEAR functions extract the relevant portions of a date (which may be held either in date format or as a number). WEEKDAY returns the day of the week (as a number) for any date: 1 is Sunday, 7 is Saturday.

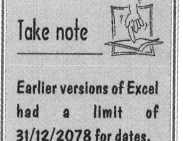

Take note

Earlier versions of Excel had a limit of 31/12/2078 for dates.

The following functions can be used to derive values from the system clock:

- ☐ TODAY returns the current date.

- ☐ NOW returns the current date and time.

In a similar way, time of day is stored as a number in the range 0 to 1, with the value representing the portion of the day that has elapsed. So 6 am is represented by 0.25, midday is 0.5 and midnight is 0.

Numbers and times (including AM and PM if required) can be interchanged by applying numeric or time formats.

You can also combine a date and time; the part to the left of the decimal place represents the date, that to the right represents the time. For instance, 35065.25 represents 1-Jan-1996 6:00 AM.

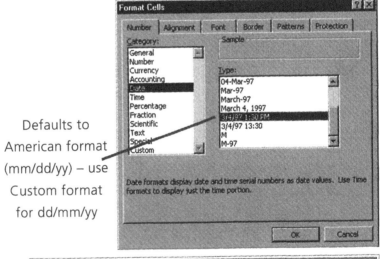

Defaults to American format (mm/dd/yy) – use Custom format for dd/mm/yy

Tip

Use NOW on sheets that are to be printed out. The current date and time are updated whenever the sheet is loaded or recalculated.

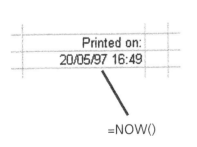

Printed on:
20/05/97 16:49

=NOW()

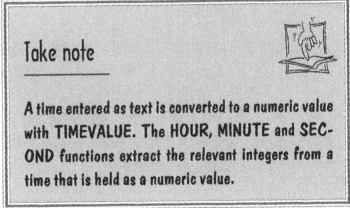

Take note

A time entered as text is converted to a numeric value with TIMEVALUE. The HOUR, MINUTE and SEC-OND functions extract the relevant integers from a time that is held as a numeric value.

Custom formats

Digits

You can create your own customised formats. Select Format |Cells and click on the Custom tab. Either choose one of the existing formats and edit it, or create your own format in the Type box.

The format consists of up to four sections, separated by semicolons:

- The format for positive numbers

- The format for negative numbers

- The format for zero

- The format for text entered in the cell

Each part of the format is made up of a series of special codes. In particular, you can use symbols such as £ and %, or full stop as the decimal point. Negative values should be preceded or followed by a minus sign, or enclosed in brackets. The digits of the number are represented by #, 0 or ? symbols.

If any part of the format is omitted, the display is blank for corresponding values.

The format characters for digits have the following meaning:

- ☐ A digit represented by # will not be displayed if it is zero (when at the beginning or end of the number).

- ☐ A digit represented by 0 is always displayed, even when zero.

- ☐ A ? after the decimal point displays a space if the digit is zero and at the end of the number (so the decimal points will still line up).

If there are more digits to the right of the decimal place than there are format characters, the number is rounded; if there are insufficient format characters to the left, the complete number is shown anyway.

Take note

Custom date and time formats can be created using d, m, y, h, m and s components. The Custom category has several alternatives, which can be further customised.

Text

- Text in number formats must always be in quotes.

- An @ symbol is replaced by the actual text entered in the cell.

- You can include fixed or variable text in any part of the format.

The format in the illustration is as follows:

£#0.00;-£#0.00;"Nil";"Invalid: "@

This is interpreted as follows:

- Positive numbers have a leading £ sign, at least one digit before the decimal point and always two decimal places.

- Negative numbers have a minus sign.

- Zero values are shown as the text 'Nil'.

- Text entries are displayed as the word 'Invalid:' followed by the actual text entered.

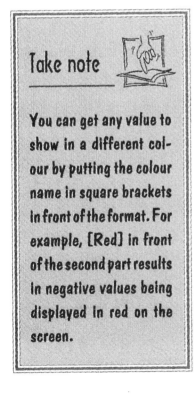

Take note

You can get any value to show in a different colour by putting the colour name in square brackets in front of the format. For example, [Red] in front of the second part results in negative values being displayed in red on the screen.

Sample output based on first cell in range

Enter custom format codes here

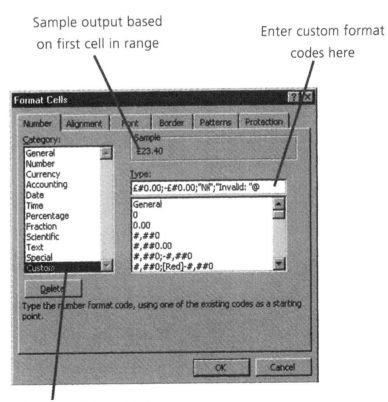

New format will be added to this category

Summary of Section 8

- [ ] Dates are stored as whole numbers, counting from 31/12/1899 up to 31/12/9999.

- [ ] Times are stored as decimals in the range 0 to 1, representing the proportion of the day that has elapsed.

- [ ] A single floating point number can represent a combined date and time.

- [ ] Customised display formats can be designed, consisting of four parts: positive numbers, negative numbers, zero, text.

- [ ] Customised formats can also be created for dates and times.

9 Formatting a worksheet

Column width and row height

Entering values and formulae is only the start of using a worksheet. Usually, you will be aiming to produce some type of report from the worksheet or, at the very least, will want to improve the layout of the sheet for your own benefit.

The first stage is to change the widths of the columns to make them more suitable for the data they contain. By default, each column starts with a column width of about nine numeric characters. You can change this default – so that all columns take this new width – or you can adjust individual columns.

Width options

- ☐ Select Format | Column | Standard Width to set a new default width.

- ☐ Click on a cell or mark a range and then select Format | Column | Width to change the width of one or more columns.

- ☐ Select Format | Column | AutoFit Selection to make the width of one or more columns automatically adjust to fit the longest item of data in each case.

Column width is given in terms of the average number of characters in the standard font

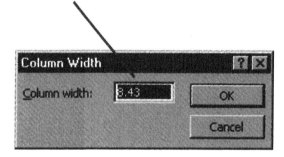

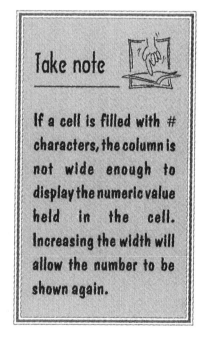

Take note

If a cell is filled with # characters, the column is not wide enough to display the numeric value held in the cell. Increasing the width will allow the number to be shown again.

Height options

- Select Format|Row|Height to change the height of a single row or a highlighted series of rows.

- Select Format | Row | Autofit to make the height of the rows adjust to fit their contents.

In a similar way to the width, you can adjust the height of each row. This will be necessary if you change the fonts, use multi-line text, or simply want to put a bigger gap between sections of the worksheet.

Row height is given in points; there are 72 points per inch. The standard font uses 10-point text.

Shortcuts

- The quickest way to change the width of one column is to drag the right-hand edge of the column border (next to the column letter). To make a column fit the widest item of data, double-click on the column border.

- The easiest way to change the height of a row is to drag the bottom edge of the row border (immediately below the row number).

Double-click on border to fit widest item in column B

Drag here to change width of column A

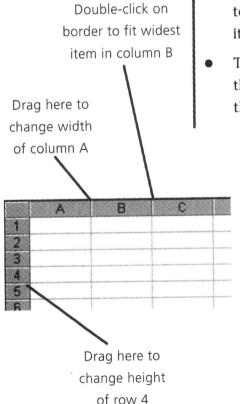

Drag here to change height of row 4

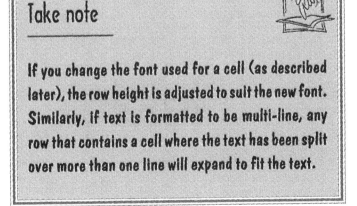

Take note

If you change the font used for a cell (as described later), the row height is adjusted to suit the new font. Similarly, if text is formatted to be multi-line, any row that contains a cell where the text has been split over more than one line will expand to fit the text.

Alignment

When data is first entered, text is placed on the left of the cell and numbers line up on the right. Numbers can be tidied up by applying a suitable format: for example, a fixed number of decimal places. For most purposes this is satisfactory but there are times when you need the text to be aligned to the right of the cell or numbers on the left.

The Format|Cells command has an Alignment tab that allows you to change the position of data in any cell. As a shortcut, four of the buttons on the toolbar can be used to apply a new alignment to the range that is currently highlighted.

The Alignment options also allow you to display text at an angle.

Basic steps

1 Mark the cell or range to be re-aligned.

2 Select Cells from the Format menu.

3 Click on the Alignment tab.

4 Choose Left, Center or Right alignment.

Or:

1 Mark the cell or range to be re-aligned.

2 Click on the appropriate button on the toolbar.

This text is left aligned	This text is centred	This text is right aligned

Left aligned   Centred   Right aligned

Click to change angle

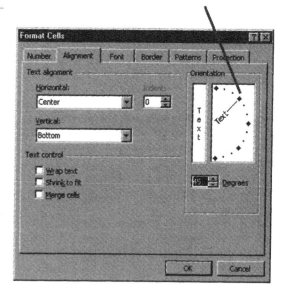

Merge and Center

74

Basic steps

To centre a piece of text over more than one column:

1 Type the text into the left-hand column.

2 Mark a range, starting with the text cell and extending over the cells in which the text is to be centred. (All cells in the range must be empty.)

3 Select Format | Cells and choose Center Across Selection from the Alignment tab.

You can also use the Merge and Center button on the toolbar but this has a more permanent effect, merging the selected cells into a single cell.

Text can spread over more than one column or row.

● If you type text into a cell that is too narrow, and the cell to the right is empty, the text will spread over both columns on the display.

● Text can be **centred** over a group of cells, providing these are all blank, by clicking on the Center Across Selection button.

● Text can be made to **wrap** over multiple lines within a cell, using the Wrap Text option from the Alignment tab. Any words that will not fit on one line are carried over to the next line and the height of the row adjusts to take all the text.

● Text that has been wrapped in a cell can be **justified**, so that there is a straight right-hand margin, using the Justify option from the Alignment tab.

Take note

Text will only spread into the next column or be centred over columns if the neighbouring cells are completely empty. Clearing them by pressing the space bar is not enough; use Edit | Clear instead.

Although text may be displayed in several columns, it is still held in its original cell as far as Excel is concerned.

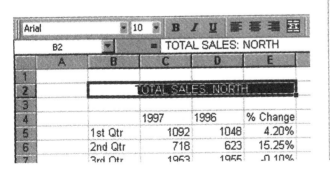

Inserting rows and columns

You should always design the layout of the worksheet before you start to put anything on the computer but, inevitably, there will be times when you don't get it right first time. You can delete or move the contents of cells without any difficulty and you may also need to insert or delete rows or columns.

New rows are inserted above the current row, new columns to the left of the current column, using the Insert menu.

Basic steps

1 Click on any cell in the row above which the new row is to be inserted or in the column to the left of which the new column is required.

2 Select Rows or Columns from the Insert menu.

To insert more than one row or column, highlight the required number of cells before choosing the command. For instance, to insert three blank columns, start by marking a range that covers three existing columns.

Insert rows

Insert columns

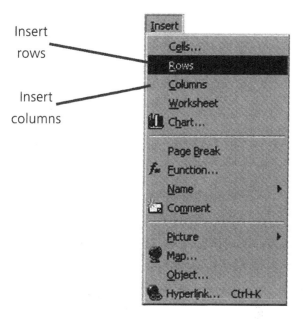

Take note

All new columns have the same width and format as the column to the left.

All formulae are updated so that they still relate to the same cells as before (regardless of whether the references were relative or absolute).

Basic steps

1 Mark a range that covers all the rows or columns to be deleted.

2 Select Delete from the Edit menu; the Delete dialogue box appears.

3 Click on Entire Row to delete one or more rows, Entire Column for the columns.

Rows and columns are erased from the worksheet with frightening simplicity. The Edit | Delete command lets you cut out any section of the sheet.

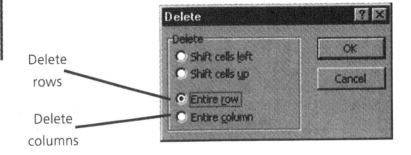

Delete rows

Delete columns

Tip

Always save the worksheet with [Ctrl]+ [S] before deleting anything; it is very easy to make mistakes and deletions cannot always be undone.

Take note

After a deletion, all rows and columns are renumbered and all formulae are revised so that they still refer to the same cells. If you delete a row or column that is part of a range reference, the formula will adjust; however, if you delete the whole of a range reference or an individual cell reference, the result of the formula will be #REF!

Inserting and deleting cells

You can achieve most effects by inserting and deleting rows and columns, moving or copying ranges, or combining these operations. Sometimes it is a useful shortcut to be able to insert or delete ranges of cells.

When you insert cells, all cells to the right or below move left or down to make space for them. The contents of other rows and columns are not affected.

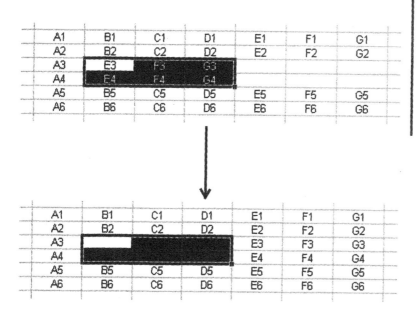

Inserting

1 Mark a range of cells. The top left-hand corner of the range determines the insertion point; the size of the range determines how much of the sheet will be affected and how many cells will be inserted.

2 Select Cells from the Insert menu.

3 Click on Shift Cells Right or Shift Cells Down, depending on the direction you want the range to move.

Move cells in selected rows to the right

Move cells in selected columns down

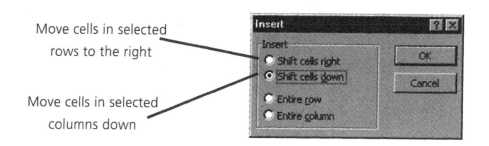

78

Deleting

1 Mark a range of cells to be deleted.

2 Select Delete from the Edit menu.

3 Click on Shift Cells Left or Shift Cells Up, depending on how you want to fill the gap.

Inserting and deleting cells requires more thought than other, similar operations and most of the time you will stick to column and row actions. However, the cell operations are particularly useful where a group of values are in the wrong row or column.

Move cells in selected rows to the left

Move cells in selected columns up

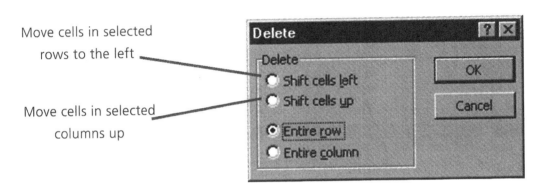

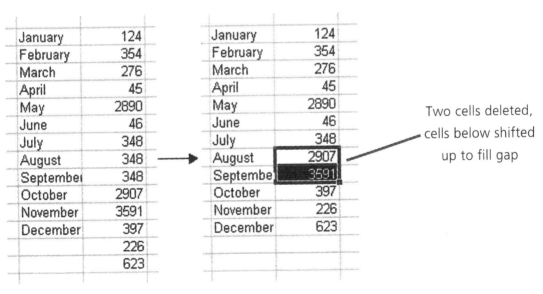

Two cells deleted, cells below shifted up to fill gap

Fixing titles

On large worksheets, you may need to be able to see the titles at the top of the sheet, or the row headings on the left, when you are working with data at some distant point. You can do this by **freezing** the titles.

The Window|Freeze Panes command allows you to fix the rows above the current cell so that they will no longer scroll out of view. However, if you move the cursor to the right, they will still scroll right. Similarly, the columns to the left are fixed and will only scroll up and down.

To free the titles again, select Window|Unfreeze Panes.

1 Click on the cell in the top-left corner of the area that is to move freely (e.g. cell C5).

2 Select Window|Freeze Panes.

You can now move anywhere on the sheet (including the title areas) but the titles will always be visible. In the example, columns A and B are fixed, as are rows 1 to 4.

Tip

To fix rows only, put the cursor in column A; to fix columns only, put the cursor in row 1.

Completely fixed

Scrolls horizontally

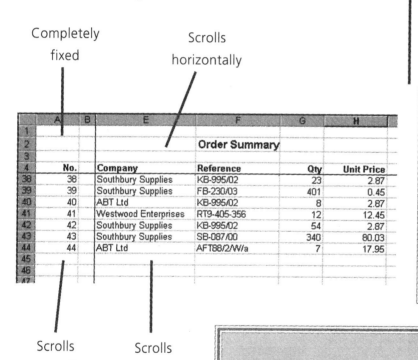

	A	B	E	F	G	H
1						
2				Order Summary		
3						
4	No.		Company	Reference	Qty	Unit Price
38	38		Southbury Supplies	KB-995/02	23	2.87
39	39		Southbury Supplies	FB-230/03	401	0.45
40	40		ABT Ltd	KB-995/02	8	2.87
41	41		Westwood Enterprises	RT9-405-356	12	12.45
42	42		Southbury Supplies	KB-995/02	54	2.87
43	43		Southbury Supplies	SB-087/00	340	80.03
44	44		ABT Ltd	AFT88/2/W/a	7	17.95
45						
46						
47						

Scrolls vertically

Scrolls normally

Take note

The Window|Split command divides the sheet into two or four areas, in a similar way, but any of these can be scrolled independently of the others.

Basic steps

1 Mark the cells in which data entry is to be allowed. (Click on the column letter or row number to mark whole columns or rows.)

2 Select Format | Cells | Protection and clear the Locked box.

3 Repeat for any other ranges that are not to be protected.

4 Select Tools | Protection | Protect Sheet. Enter a password if required (making sure Caps Lock is off).

Clear the protection with Tools | Protection | Unprotect Sheet.

Much of the sheet will contain data that is to be derived from formulae and therefore must not be changed directly. You can protect the worksheet against alterations, so that data is entered only in certain areas.

The Tools menu contains an option to protect the entire sheet against change. Before choosing this option, you must identify those areas of the sheet where changes are to be allowed. Users of the sheet will then not be able to overwrite data accidentally.

If you apply a password, users will have to enter the correct password before any changes can be made.

Clear for unprotected cells

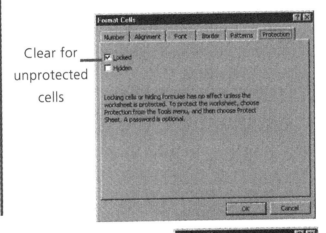

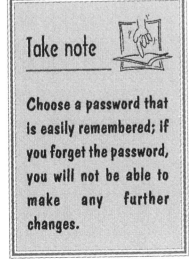

Take note

Choose a password that is easily remembered; if you forget the password, you will not be able to make any further changes.

Select types of data to protect

Enter password if required

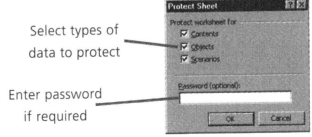

Message when attempting to enter data in protected area

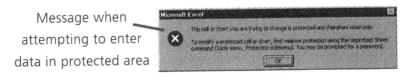

Summary of Section 9

- ❑ The width of any column can be changed with the Format | Column command or by dragging the divider between column letters.

- ❑ The height of any row is changed with Format | Row or by dragging the divider between row numbers.

- ❑ Text can be aligned to left or right of the cell, or centred within the cell or across a series of cells.

- ❑ New rows or columns can be inserted with the Insert menu, or deleted with the Edit | Delete command.

- ❑ Blocks of cells can also be inserted or deleted (though moving blocks is preferable).

- ❑ Titles can be fixed with the Window | Freeze Panes command, so that they are always visible, no matter where you are in the sheet.

- ❑ The worksheet can be protected against change with Tools | Protection | Protect Sheet. Areas where data entry is to be allowed must be marked first with Format | Cells | Protection.

10 Cosmetics

Changing fonts

The **font** is the style of text used to display the contents of cells (both text and numeric values). A font is defined by the following characteristics:

- The typeface (e.g. Arial, Times and Courier)

- The point size (e.g. 8 point, 10 point and 12 point)

- The attributes (e.g. **bold**, *italic* and underline)

Fonts are applied to cells and ranges in a similar way to other characteristics, such as alignment. Although you can use the Font tab from the Format | Cells command, the easiest way is to use the buttons on the toolbar.

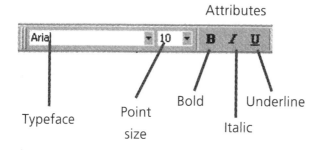

Attributes

Typeface   Point size   Bold   Italic   Underline

Take note

Points are the most common units for measuring text size. There are 72 points to the inch for printed text. The point size is the height of the text line, usually from the bottom of any descender (as on g and y) to the top of capital letters. The measurement excludes the leading (the blank space between lines of text).

Basic steps

To change the font for cells:

1 Select the cell or range to which the new font is to be applied.

2 Click on the arrow to the right of the typeface box on the toolbar and click on the required typeface from the drop-down list.

3 In a similar way, select the point size (or simply type the size directly into the Points box).

4 Click on the bold, italic or underline buttons to change the attributes. Each time you click a button, the attribute is turned on or off. Any combination of attributes is allowed.

84

Basic steps

To change the font for a group of characters:

1 Double-click on the cell containing the text (for text centred across columns, the left-hand cell of the range).

2 Drag the pointer over the characters to be changed, highlighting them.

3 Select the typeface, size and attributes, as before.

The following keys can be used as shortcuts for the attributes:

[Ctrl]+[B]	Bold
[Ctrl]+[I]	Italic
[Ctrl]+[U]	Underline

For cells formatted as numbers or dates, the font applies to all the characters in the cell. For text cells, however, you can format individual characters and groups of characters. This allows you to produce a mixture of fonts within a cell and is particularly useful for headings.

	A	B	C	D	E	F
1						
2			**TOTAL SALES: NORTH**			
3						
4			1997	1996	% Change	
5		1st Qtr	1092	1048	4.20%	
6		2nd Qtr	718	623	15.25%	
7		3rd Qtr	1053	1055	0.10%	

22 point bold   14 point bold   10 point right-aligned

Take note

If you increase the font size, the row expands to accommodate the new height.

Tip

Use fonts sparingly; too many fonts on a worksheet or printed report look untidy and detract from the information you are trying to present. Apply different fonts to emphasise and enhance titles and results but keep the number of variations to a minimum.

Borders, patterns and colours

For further enhancement of your work, and to highlight particular blocks of data or subdivide complicated tables, Excel provides a range of features for drawing boxes, shading cells and changing the colours.

Click here to apply   Click here to change

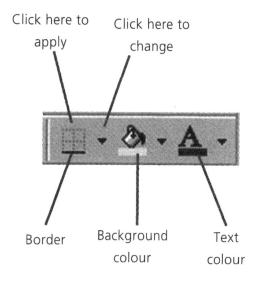

Border   Background colour   Text colour

Click

Border options

Options

There are two ways of changing these features for the current cell or a highlighted range:

☐ Select the Format | Cells command, then click on the Border tab or Patterns tab.

☐ Click on the arrows to the right of the border, background colour and text colour buttons on the toolbar, then select from the drop-down lists.

When a border, colour or pattern has been chosen, it can be applied to further cells or ranges by selecting the area to be changed and clicking on the appropriate button.

> **Tip**
>
> **Borders and patterns are best applied when the substance of the worksheet is complete. You can waste a lot of time adding and changing borders if you do so while the sheet is under development.**

Borders, patterns and colours can be applied to individual cells or ranges.

- To draw a border around a block of cells, highlight the entire block, then choose the border.

- To divide columns with vertical lines, mark each column separately and apply a border on the right (or left).

- To box individual cells, each cell must be given its own border.

The background colour is applied to whole cells. As for fonts, the text colour can be changed for individual characters in a text cell but must be applied to the entire cell for numbers and dates.

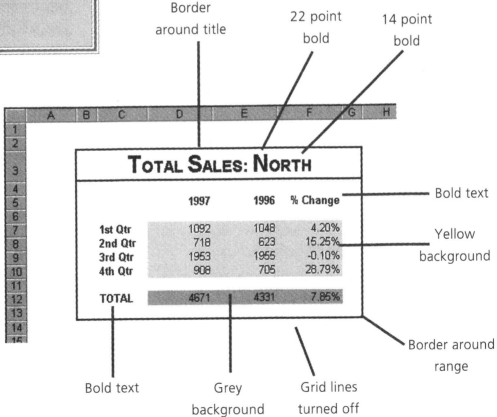

Border around title

22 point bold

14 point bold

Bold text

Yellow background

Bold text

Grey background

Grid lines turned off

Border around range

TOTAL SALES: NORTH

	1997	1996	% Change
1st Qtr	1092	1048	4.20%
2nd Qtr	718	623	15.25%
3rd Qtr	1953	1955	-0.10%
4th Qtr	908	705	28.79%
TOTAL	4671	4331	7.85%

Hiding rows and columns

The results produced on worksheets often require a series of steps, with one or more intermediate values. These extra cells may clutter the display and be of no interest in themselves, once the sheet is working satisfactorily. These values can be placed in separate rows and columns, which can then be **hidden**.

The effect of hiding a row or column is purely that it does not appear on the display or in printouts; the formulae in hidden rows and columns still work in exactly the same way and there is no effect on the results.

Columns F and
G hidden

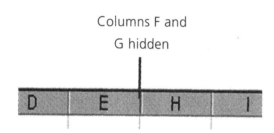

To hide rows or columns:

1 Mark a range that covers at least one cell in each of the rows or columns to be hidden.

2 Select Format | Row | Hide or Format | Column | Hide.

To redisplay rows or columns:

1 Click on the border between adjacent cells (where the row or column will reappear).

2 Select Format | Row | Unhide or Format | Column | Unhide.

Take note

The title bar, toolbars and status bar can be hidden (or redisplayed) using View|Full Screen. The Row & Column Header option in the View tab of the Tools|Options command hides the row letters and column numbers.

Tip

You can tell when there are hidden rows or columns on a worksheet because there will be a jump in the row numbers or column letters.

Basic steps

To copy a format:

1 Click on the cell whose format is to be copied.

2 Click on the Format Painter button.

3 Mark the range that is to receive the new format.

When the mouse button is released, the new format is applied to all the highlighted cells, replacing whatever was there before.

You can undo mistakes in formatting with **[Ctrl]+[Z]**.

Once you have created a format for one cell, you can easily copy this to any other range on the worksheet using the Format Painter. This will apply the same number/text format, alignment, font, border, pattern and colour to all selected cells.

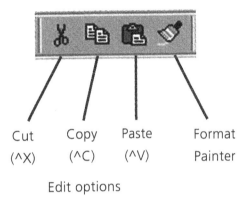

Cut   Copy   Paste   Format
(^X)   (^C)   (^V)   Painter

Edit options

Tip

To copy the format to several ranges, double-click on the Format Painter button. After copying the format, click the button again.

Take note

You can also copy the formats from one range to another, providing they have a similar layout. For example, the formats for the first row of the original block will be copied to the first row of the new block. However, the result may not always be as you expect, so always save the worksheet first.

Format styles

For simple sheets and one-off applications, the ability to copy formats between cells is all you need. For more complex applications, however, it is useful to give names to the format combinations you use.

A **style** is a combination of number/text format, alignment, font, border, pattern, colour and protection status. All you have to do is give the style a name, and this can be applied to any other range in the worksheet.

The use of styles is particularly important when you are creating a series of worksheets or wish to devise a company standard to be used by a number of people.

Enter new style name

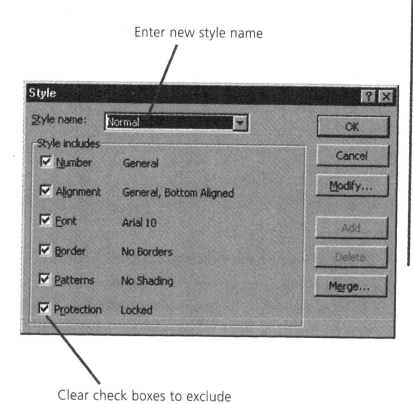

Clear check boxes to exclude
items from style

1 Apply the necessary formatting to an individual cell.

2 With the cell highlighted, select Format | Style and enter a new name in the Style box.

3 You can restrict the style to just some of the formatting features. For instance, you may set up a style for everything except the number format; all cells with this style will have the same appearance (font, alignment etc.) but can have different number formats.

4 Click on OK when the style is complete or Cancel to abandon.

90

Take note

The Normal style is the default style that is applied to all new styles. You cannot delete the style but you can modify it, changing all new cells and any that do not have another style attached.

When a style has been defined, you can use it as follows:

- To apply a style to a range of cells, highlight the range and then click on the required style in the Style box of the Format | Style window. Any existing formatting on the cells is lost.

- After applying a style, individual formatting elements can be changed (for instance, you can change the colour of a cell but the other style elements stay the same).

- To change a style, select Format | Style, choose the style from the drop-down list and click on Modify. Then update any part of the style. When you click on OK, all cells that have this style are updated (except where the style has been overridden by manual changes).

- To delete a style, select Format | Style, choose the style and click on Delete. Any cells with this style have the style removed (effectively, they are given the Normal style) but any later formatting that was added still applies.

Tip

You can add a Style box to a toolbar using Tools | Customize; click on the Commands tab, select the Format category and drag the Style box to the required position. Styles can then be selected by clicking on this box; you can add a new style by typing it directly into the Style box.

Style box added to formatting toolbar

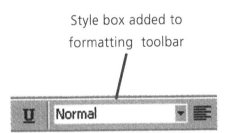

Summary of Section 10

- ❑ The **font** is the style of text, consisting of typeface, point size and attributes (bold, italic, underline).

- ❑ Any font can be applied to a cell and, in text cells, individual characters can be given different fonts. Each numeric or date cell can have only one font.

- ❑ Borders can be drawn around cells and ranges, which can also be given a background of a different pattern or colour. The colour of text can also be changed.

- ❑ In text cells, individual characters can be different colours; each numeric or date cell can have only one colour.

- ❑ Rows and columns can be hidden from view but their formulae will still be calculated in the usual way.

- ❑ The grid lines, toolbars and borders can also be hidden.

- ❑ The Format Painter is used to copy the format of a cell to other cells; features copied include the number format, alignment, font, border, pattern, colour and protection status.

- ❑ Formats can be named to produce **styles**. A named style can be applied to any cell or range.

11 Workbooks

Multiple worksheets

So far, we have considered just a single worksheet. Excel allows you to have several worksheets in a single file, which is referred to as a **workbook**. A workbook may also contain other types of sheet and Visual Basic macros for automating tasks.

Whenever you save the file, **all** sheets in the workbook will be saved together. Similarly, loading a file loads into memory **all** the sheets in the workbook.

The sheets are shown in the sheet tabs at the bottom of the window.

The sheets in a workbook can be of two different types:

- ☐ **Worksheets**, for the entry of data and formulae and the calculation of results

- ☐ **Chart sheets**, for the display of graphs and charts (see page 116)

Current sheet

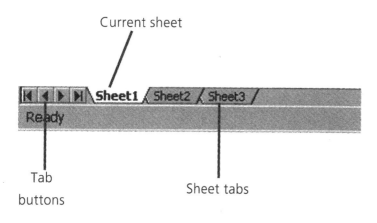

Tab buttons

Sheet tabs

Take note

Previous versions of Excel allowed Visual Basic sheets and Dialogue sheets. These are now accessed with the Visual Basic Editor – see page 142.

Tip

Only include worksheets in a workbook if there is going to be some beneficial effect from doing so. For instance, if data from one sheet is used on another sheet or a series of sheets are always printed together in a report, then it is worth putting them all in the same workbook. However, if a number of worksheets are similar but not related in any other way, they are probably better saved in separate files; otherwise you are just making matters more complicated unnecessarily.

Basic steps

To rename a sheet in a workbook:

1 Double-click on the sheet tab at the bottom of the window.

2 Enter a new name in the sheet tab; the name can be up to 31 characters long, using any characters, including spaces.

3 Click on OK. The new name is shown in the sheet tab, which expands to show the full name.

You can also rename sheets with Format | Sheet | Rename.

Each sheet in the workbook has a tab at the bottom of the window. Initially the sheets are called Sheet1, Sheet2 etc. but these names can be changed to something more meaningful.

By default, Excel gives you three sheets for each workbook but this number can be increased when necessary – see page 100.

The View Tab for Tools | Options changes the way in which worksheets are displayed. Some of these features relate to the current worksheet only; others affect the whole workbook.

Sheet1 renamed as Summary

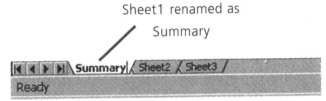

Whole workbook

Current worksheet only

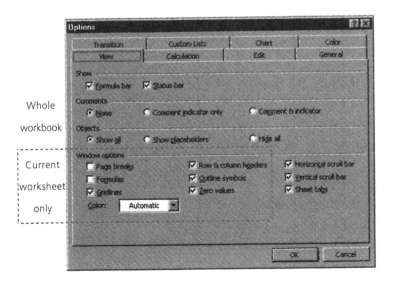

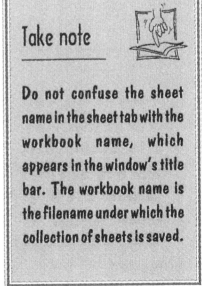

Take note

Do not confuse the sheet name in the sheet tab with the workbook name, which appears in the window's title bar. The workbook name is the filename under which the collection of sheets is saved.

Starting a new sheet

To start a new worksheet in the workbook, simply click on any of the sheet tabs at the bottom of the window: for example, Sheet2. You will be presented with a completely blank sheet, in which a new set of data, formulae and titles can be entered.

This sheet need have no connection with any other sheet in the workbook, other than the fact that all sheets are saved and loaded together.

1 Click on a new sheet tab to display a blank worksheet.

2 Double-click on the sheet tab to change the sheet name.

3 Start entering data and formulae, then save the workbook.

When you run out of blank shets, you can insert a new one – see page 100. You can also change the order of the sheets.

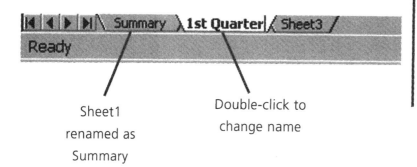

Sheet1 renamed as Summary

Double-click to change name

Tip

If there are many sheets in the workbook, it may be worth putting a menu sheet at the front of the workbook with work-sheets selected by clicking on buttons – see page 143.

Take note

If you make a major mistake in a sheet (for example, deleting the wrong range of cells), you should undo the error with [Ctrl]+[Z] immediately. Alternatively, close and re-open the file, restoring the file to the state it was in when you last saved it. Otherwise, if you move to another sheet, make changes and save the file, your mistakes in the other sheet will also be saved.

Scroll buttons

The four scroll buttons work as follows:

☐ The left button displays the first sheet tab.

☐ The second button displays the previous tab on the left.

☐ The third button displays the next tab on the right.

☐ The last button displays the last sheet tab in the workbook.

You can switch from one sheet to another simply by clicking on the sheet tabs at the bottom of the window. When a tab is clicked, the corresponding sheet is displayed in the window and the sheet name is highlighted on the tab.

When you have a number of sheets, you will not be able to see all the tabs. The tabs can be scrolled to the left or right with the small tab buttons. Clicking on these buttons only moves the tabs; it does not select a different sheet.

The bar along the bottom is shared by the sheet tabs and the horizontal scroll bars. You can change the amount used for each by dragging the divider to the left or right.

First   Next

|◄ ◄ ► ►| **Summary** ╱ 1st Quarter ╱ 2nd Quarter ╱ 3rd Quarter ╱ 4th Quarter ╱ Sale |◄ |

Last
Previous

Drag to change
share of bar

Take note

When you select a different sheet, any changes you have made to the other sheets are not lost; the data is still held in memory. When you save the workbook, the contents of all sheets are saved.

Tip

Include the sheet name in a title cell, so that you can always see at a glance which sheet you are working on (particularly when the workbook contains several similar sheets). Otherwise, the sheet tab may be the only way of identifying the current sheet and this is not included when the file is printed.

Multiple windows

You can display more than one worksheet from the file at a time by opening new windows onto the workbook. Select the Window | New Window command and the effect is that a second window is opened, showing the same sheet.

The windows can be resized or moved to show data in the most convenient form, using the usual Windows actions (see page 101). You may also need to change the size of the windows with the View | Zoom options.

These windows can be used independently. They show two different parts of the same worksheet or two different sheets from the workbook. You can enter data and formulae into either sheet. When you save the workbook, any changes made in either window are saved.

When you close the workbook (with File | Exit or by clicking on Close in the control menu) all subsidiary windows are closed. If any data has not been saved, you are given the opportunity to do so.

Options

- You will not be able to view multiple sheets if the sheet window is maximised: click on the Maximise button to reduce the size.

- Use the Window | Arrange command to re-arrange multiple windows.

Take note

If the two sheets show some of the same cells, any change in these cells in one window will be reflected in the cells of the other window.

Tip

Although you can have several windows open at once, keep the number to a minimum. When there are too many windows, the screen becomes unnecessarily complicated.

Take note

You can also use File | Open to open a second workbook and display the worksheets from two workbooks side by side.

Basic steps

To mark a group of consecutive sheets:

1 Click on the first sheet tab.

2 Hold down the **[Shift]** key.

3 Click on the last sheet tab in the group.

To mark non-consecutive sheets:

1 Click on the first sheet tab.

2 Hold down the **[Ctrl]** key.

3 Click each of the other tabs in turn (clicking on the same tab a second time removes it from the group).

To cancel the selection, just click on a single tab without holding **[Shift]** or **[Ctrl]**.

Worksheet groups

Sometimes you will want to work with more than one sheet at a time. For instance, you may want to put the same title in a series of sheets, or the row and column headings may be the same across all sheets.

A group of sheets can be selected: either a group of consecutive sheets or a selection of non-adjacent sheets. Any entry made in the current sheet will then be repeated in the corresponding cell in all other sheets in the group. This gives you a quick way of filling a series of sheets.

Take note

If you have entered the same value in several sheets, you can then edit any of the individual sheets without affecting the others (providing the group is no longer selected).

Tip

If two or more sheets have similar entries, it is often quicker to enter the same value in all sheets and then edit some of them, than to enter each individually.

Changing sheets

You are free to insert new sheets, copy sheets, change the order of sheets and delete unwanted sheets.

To insert a new sheet, click on one of the sheet tabs and then select the appropriate command from the Insert menu (e.g. Insert|Worksheet for a new worksheet). The worksheet is inserted to the left of the selected sheet and becomes the active sheet.

You can add several worksheets at once by selecting the corresponding number of existing sheet tabs. For example, to insert three new sheets, first select a group of three existing tabs.

To delete an unwanted sheet, click on the sheet tab and then select Edit|Delete Sheet. (Always save the workbook first, in case you make a mistake.)

Insert options

New sheets are inserted as follows:

☐ By selecting the Insert | Worksheet command to add a new worksheet

☐ By clicking on the As New Sheet button in the final step when defining a chart (see page 111).

Charts on worksheets can also be converted to separate chart sheets (see page 116).

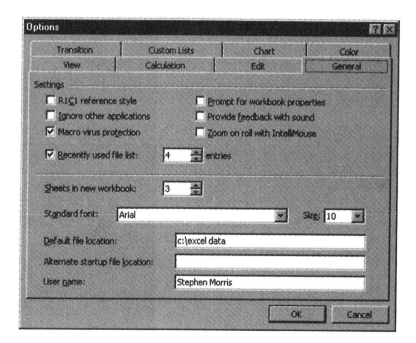

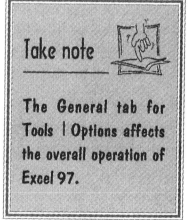

Take note

The General tab for Tools | Options affects the overall operation of Excel 97.

100

Take note

The new order of sheets is only saved permanently when you save the workbook.

To move a sheet to a different position in the workbook, click on the sheet tab and then drag it across the tabs to its new position.

To make a copy of a sheet in the same workbook, click on the sheet tab, press and hold **[Ctrl]**, and then drag the tab to the point at which you want to insert the copy sheet.

You can move or copy a number of sheets if you start by marking a group of tabs.

First open window

Second open window

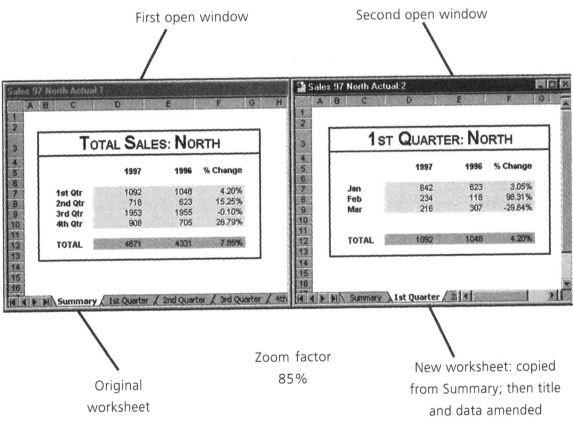

Original worksheet

Zoom factor 85%

New worksheet: copied from Summary; then title and data amended

Formulae across worksheets

A formula can refer to cells and ranges in other worksheets, or even a three-dimensional range covering several worksheets.

To reference a cell in another sheet, precede the cell reference with the sheet name and an exclamation mark. For instance, the summary sheet will include the value from cell D12 in the 1st Quarter worksheet if cell D7 contains the formula:

='1st Quarter'!D12

When this formula is copied to other cells, it is updated like any other relative reference (e.g. the value in E7 is '1st Quarter'!E12).

A formula may also refer to a range in another sheet:

=SUM('1st Quarter'!D7:D9)

This formula adds the contents of all cells in the range D7:D9 in the 1st Quarter sheet, putting the answer in the selected cell of the current sheet.

To enter the total in D7 of the Summary sheet:

1 Display two windows for the workbook, one showing the Summary sheet, the other the 1st Quarter sheet.

2 Click on D7 in the Summary sheet.

3 Type = in the cell.

4 Click on the 1st Quarter sheet and then on D12 in that sheet; the formula is updated as you do so.

5 Press **[Enter]**.

Any change in D7, D8 or D9 in the 1st Quarter sheet results in a corresponding change in D7 in the Summary sheet.

Take note

If you insert or delete rows and columns in one sheet, the formulae in other sheets are updated accordingly.

A formula can refer to a three-dimensional block of cells that covers two or more consecutive sheets. The range of sheets is placed before the exclamation mark, the range of cells after it.

For example, the grand total of sales in the Summary sheet could just as well have been calculated by:

=SUM('1st Quarter:4th Quarter'!D7:D9)

This will add the contents of all cells in the range D7:D9 in all sheets from 1st Quarter to 4th Quarter. In three-dimensional references, the same range of cells is used in all sheets. If you think of the sheets as lying one above another, this effectively gives you a three-dimensional rectangular block of cells.

If a sheet name uses characters other than numbers and letters (e.g. 1st Quarter), any sheet reference must be enclosed in single quotes. The quotes are not needed for simple names. For ranges of sheets, a single pair of quotes encloses both sheet names (as in '1st Quarter:4th Quarter').

You can also link to cells in another workbook. Open two workbooks and create the formula in the samy way as for linking across two worksheets. The formula will include the workbook name; for example:

='[Area51.xls]Totals'!$E$9

When you load a file with formulae that refer to other workbooks, you are given the opportunity to update the current values.

Summary of Section 11

❑ An Excel file is called a **workbook** and may contain many separate sheets.

❑ Each sheet is a worksheet or chart sheet.

❑ To start a new sheet, click on a sheet tab.

❑ Use the tab buttons to display further sheet tabs.

❑ Open additional windows on the sheet with Window | New Window.

❑ Open other files with File | Open.

❑ Use Window | Arrange to display multiple sheets simultaneously.

❑ Sheets can be inserted, deleted, copied and moved.

❑ Formulae can refer to ranges on other sheets or three-dimensional ranges covering several sheets.

❑ Formulae can also link to cells or ranges in other files.

12 Charts and graphics

Chart Wizard

Excel 97 provides a wide range of options for displaying any set of data as a chart or graph: bar charts, pie charts, line graphs and others. The chart can be placed anywhere on the worksheet and can be made to fit a rectangle of any size or shape. Once it has been created, any aspects of the chart can be changed. Alternatively, you can create a separate chart sheet.

A chart is created on a worksheet using the Chart Wizard which provides you with a series of dialogue boxes that are used to build up the chart.

Before starting Chart Wizard, you should mark the block of data to be charted.

Basic steps

1 Mark the range of data for which the chart is to be created. Include the row of labels above the data and the column to the left, if appropriate.

2 Click on the Chart Wizard button. The first of four dialogue boxes is displayed.

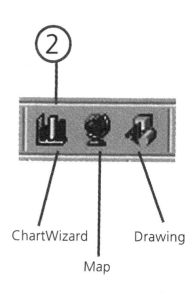

TOTAL SALES: NORTH

	1997	1996	% Change
1st Qtr	1092	1048	4.20%
2nd Qtr	718	623	15.25%
3rd Qtr	1953	1955	-0.10%
4th Qtr	908	705	28.79%
TOTAL	4671	4331	7.85%

② ChartWizard   Map   Drawing

①

Take note

You can include blank rows and columns in the range – these will be ignored. The range can be made up of non-adjacent blocks, if the data comes from different parts of the sheet.

106

3 Click on a chart type. The dialogue box shows several variations of the selected type.

4 Click on a sub-type and then on Next.

You can change the chart type after the graph has been drawn.

ChartWizard offers fifteen different types of chart. These fall into three broad categories:

● Bar charts have a rectangular bar for each item of data, the height of the bar being proportional to the data value.

● Graphs plot a series of points, with each point being determined by a pair of co-ordinates. Usually, consecutive points are joined together by a line.

● Pie charts consist of a circle divided into segments. The values in the data series are totalled, so that each value can be calculated as a percentage of the total. The sizes of the segments are proportional to these percentages.

The options provided are variations on these: for instance, three-dimensional bars or area graphs (where the value is represented by the area under the graph).

Take note

Any feature of the chart can be changed after the chart has been drawn.

Click on a chart type if you want to replace the default Column chart

Take note

The Custom Types tab has some more interesting variations.

④ Click on the sub-type

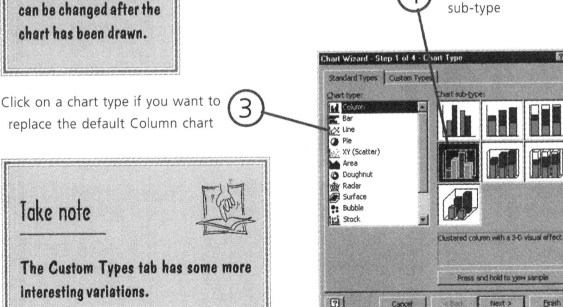

The data range consists of one or more rows or columns; each row or column will provide the data for one series of bars or for one line on a line graph.

You can choose either rows or columns for the data series. If you choose rows, the data values in each row form one set of bars or the points on one line; the column headings are the labels for the chart. If you choose columns, each column is a data series and the row headings are used as chart labels.

By columns: quarters on X-axis;
set of bars for each year

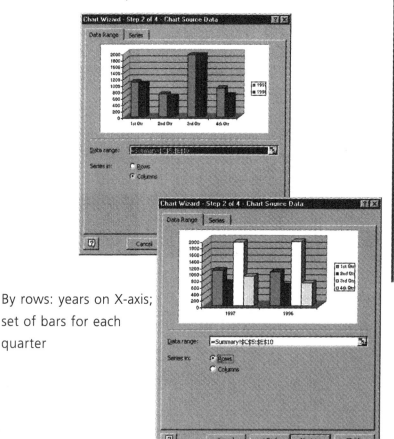

By rows: years on X-axis;
set of bars for each
quarter

5 The second dialogue box gives you the opportunity to change the data range that has been selected. You either mark the range with the pointer or edit the range in the dialogue box.

To mark a new range, click on the icon on the right of the Data Range. Mark the data area (including labels).

After marking the range, click on the icon on the right of the reduced dialogue box.

Click on Next when the range is correct.

6 Select either rows or columns as the basis for the data series.

7 Click on the Series tab and change the ranges that identify the series names, values and X-axis labels. Click on Next when the ranges are correct.

Within the data range, you should have a block of data and the labels that will be shown on the graph. The Series tab for Step 2 lets you change these ranges.

There will be one graph or one set of bars for each series. For each of these series you can identify a range containing the series name (e.g. the year) and a range of values.

The range for the X-axis labels defines the cells whose contents will be printed along the bottom of the chart.

You can mark any range by clicking on the icon to the right of the entry box.

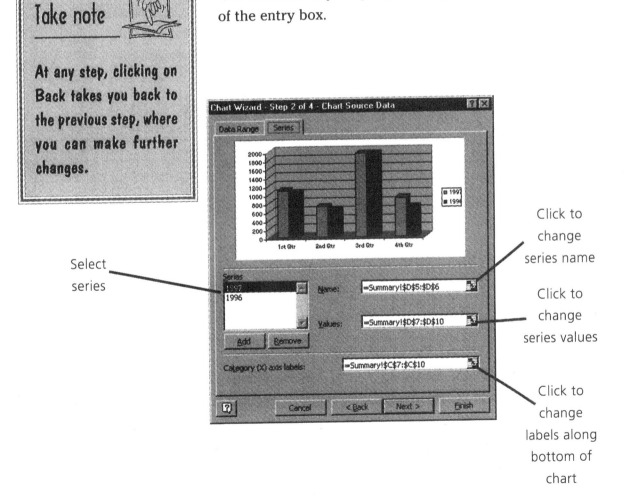

Select series

Click to change series name

Click to change series values

Click to change labels along bottom of chart

The third dialogue box lets you add explanatory text to the chart. The **chart title** is printed above the graph, and the **axis titles** are added alongside the axis labels. Other tabs let you alter other features of the chart. For example, the **legend** is a box showing the colours or types of points used for each data series.

8 Enter some text for the chart title and for each of the axes. Make any changes with the other tabs, then click on Next.

Chart title

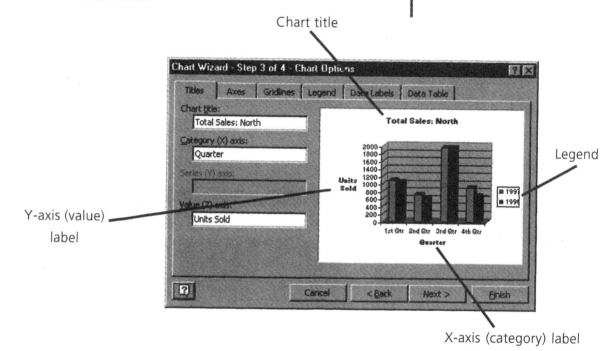

Legend

Y-axis (value) label

X-axis (category) label

Tip

Keep the titles simple and avoid cluttering the borders of the graph with too much text. If you want to add extra notes, you can use a text box - see page 120.

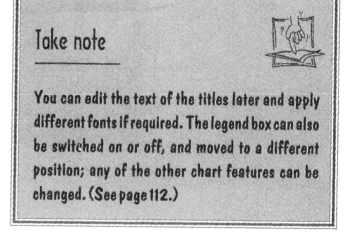

Take note

You can edit the text of the titles later and apply different fonts if required. The legend box can also be switched on or off, and moved to a different position; any of the other chart features can be changed. (See page 112.)

9 Choose the location for the chart: a separate sheet or an existing worksheet.

Click on Finish. The new chart will be displayed and can be edited if necessary.

The final dialogue box gives you the choice between overlaying the new chart on one of the worksheets (As Object In) or placing it in a new sheet (As New Sheet).

If you choose to keep the chart on an existing worksheet, you can select a different sheet from the drop-down list.

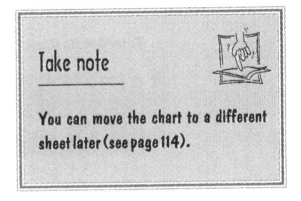

Take note

You can move the chart to a different sheet later (see page 114).

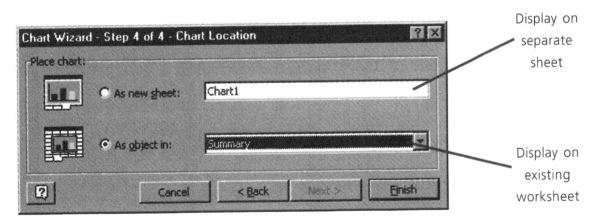

Display on separate sheet

Display on existing worksheet

Editing the chart

When the chart has been drawn, it can be moved to a new position on the sheet and can be resized to fit any reasonable gap.

If you place the mouse pointer over any part of the chart, a descriptive label pops up. If you point to a data item, the label shows you the series name and data value.

☐ To move the chart, click on it and then drag it to a new position.

☐ To change the size, click on the chart and then drag the sizing handles on the corners and sides. Hold down the **[Shift]** key while you drag to keep the proportions the same.

☐ To remove a chart from a sheet, click on the chart and press **[Delete]**.

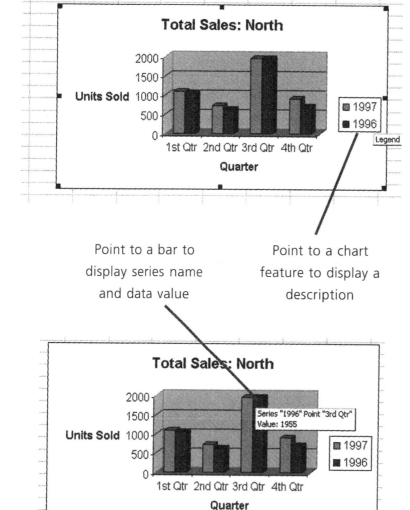

Point to a bar to display series name and data value

Point to a chart feature to display a description

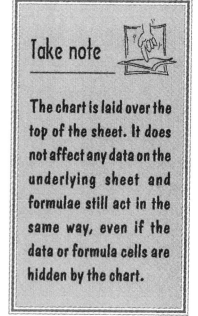

Take note

The chart is laid over the top of the sheet. It does not affect any data on the underlying sheet and formulae still act in the same way, even if the data or formula cells are hidden by the chart.

Basic steps

To edit any feature of the chart:

1 Double-click on any item on the chart: text, labels, grid lines, grid background, legend, bars or lines, etc.

2 In the dialogue box that appears, make any changes that are needed to the appearance of the chart.

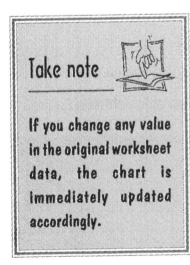
The chart produced so far was selected from only a limited number of options. You are now free to change any aspect of the chart: colours, fonts, patterns, line styles and so on.

Options for chart area
(chart background, font and general properties)

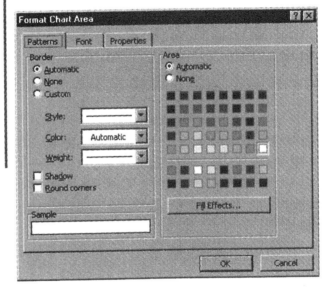

Options for axes

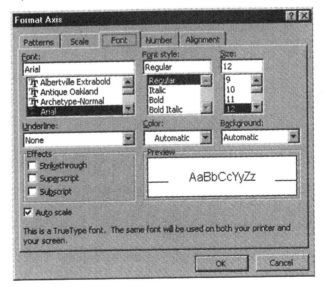

Changing chart data

You can change the range of data displayed on the chart at any time.

- New rows or columns can be added, increasing the scope of the chart.

- The range can be extended or contracted to show more or less data.

- The range can be changed completely, so that it covers a different set of data.

- Data series can be removed from the chart.

All of these tasks can be accomplished by clicking on the chart and then selecting the Chart|Source Data option. You can change the ranges for any of the series or click on Add to add a new series, Remove to delete a series from the chart. There are also alternative methods for making some of these changes.

Choose new series or
extra points for
existing series

Select direction
of data series

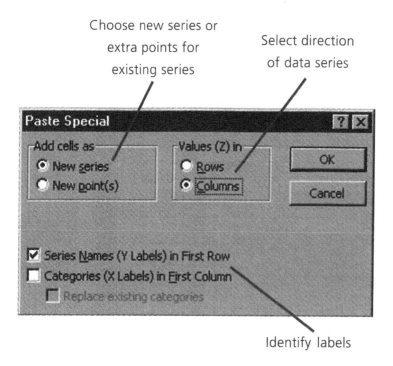

Identify labels

Alternatives

To add a new data series or extend an existing series:

1 Mark the new range (including labels).

2 Click on the range border and drag it into the chart.

3 Unless it is obvious to Excel how the data is to be displayed, you will be asked to fill in a dialogue box.

4 The chart is extended to show the new data.

To delete a data series from the chart:

1 Click on one of the bars or data points.

2 Press **[Delete]**.

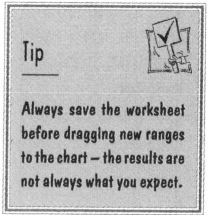

Tip

Always save the worksheet before dragging new ranges to the chart – the results are not always what you expect.

To change the view for a 3-D chart:

1 Click on the chart to select it.

2 Select 3-D View from the Chart menu.

3 To rotate the chart horizontally, click on one of the buttons below the chart.

4 To rotate the chart vertically, click on the buttons to the left of the chart.

5 Click on Apply to see the effect of the current settings and OK to finish.

When a chart has been selected by double-clicking on it, some of the menus at the top of the window change. For instance, the Insert menu allows you to insert titles, legends, data labels and grid lines; the Format menu provides a new range of options for changing the way in which the chart is displayed.

There is also a new Chart menu, replacing the Data menu. The first four options in this menu correspond to the four steps in the Chart Wizard, and bring up the same dialogue boxes.

The Chart | Add Trendline option performs regression analysis on a bar chart or graph, allowing you to predict future values by extending the trend line beyond the actual data.

The Chart | 3-D View option allows you to rotate a three-dimensional chart, both horizontally and vertically.

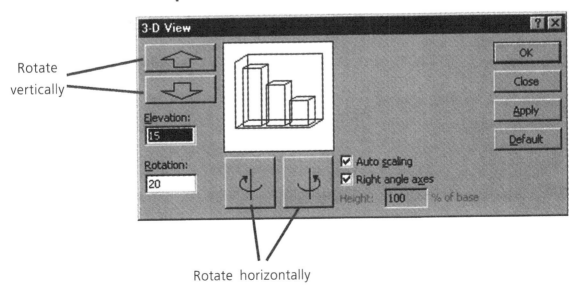

Rotate vertically

Rotate horizontally

Chart sheets

Much of the time you will include charts as part of a normal worksheet. However, you may want to use a chart as a transparency for an overhead projector, as a handout during a presentation, or simply as an individual page in a report. In these cases, you can create a separate **chart sheet** within the workbook.

The chart sheet can be created from scratch or derived from an existing chart on a worksheet.

Click to convert to chart sheet

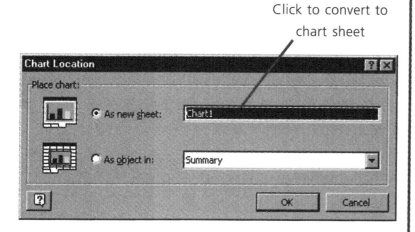

Basic steps

To create a new chart sheet:

1 Mark the range to be charted.

2 Select Chart from the Insert menu and then select As New Sheet.

3 Complete the ChartWizard dialogue boxes, as before.

The result is that a new sheet is created (this time, a chart sheet), with a default name of **Chart1**.

To convert an existing worksheet into a chart sheet:

1 Click on the chart.

2 Select Location from the Chart menu.

3 Click on As New Sheet in the Chart Location dialogue box.

4 Click on OK.

The new sheet is created and can be renamed.

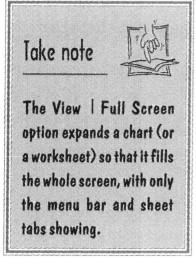

Take note

The View I Full Screen option expands a chart (or a worksheet) so that it fills the whole screen, with only the menu bar and sheet tabs showing.

Tip

You can create a chart sheet quickly, using all the default settings, by marking a range and then pressing [F11].

Options

- Rename the sheet by double-clicking on the sheet tab.

- Change the position of the sheet in the workbook by dragging the sheet tab to a new position.

- Delete the chart sheet by selecting it and then choosing Delete Sheet from the Edit menu.

The chart sheet behaves in the same way as a worksheet and is saved as part of the workbook. The chart sheet can be renamed, moved to a new position or deleted. You can also display it in a separate window or print it.

Chart sheet shown at Full Screen

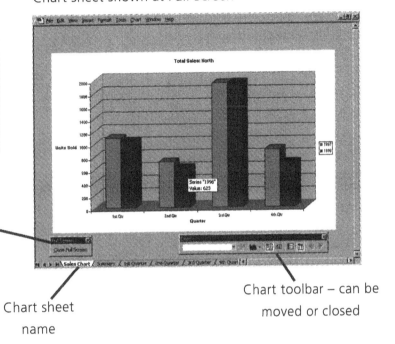

Full Screen toolbar – click button for normal vliew

Chart sheet name

Chart toolbar – can be moved or closed

Take note

You can copy a chart from a worksheet to a chart sheet. Click once on the chart (so that the sizing handles are shown at the corners) and press [Ctrl]+[C] to copy it to the clipboard; then open the chart sheet and press [Ctrl]+[V] to paste in the chart.

Similarly, you can copy a chart from a chart sheet onto a worksheet. In this case you must click in the area outside the chart, so that the sizing handles are shown on the corners of the chart sheet.

Graphic objects

Excel allows you to add lines, shapes and text to the worksheet. These objects are laid over the top of the sheet, in the same way as charts. Therefore they do not affect the data and formulae below.

Each object is a separate entity and can be manipulated independently of any other object. The objects are selected from the Drawing toolbar.

To add an object:

1 Click on the Drawing button. The toolbar is displayed.

2 Click on any shape or line on the toolbox and then mark it out on the worksheet.

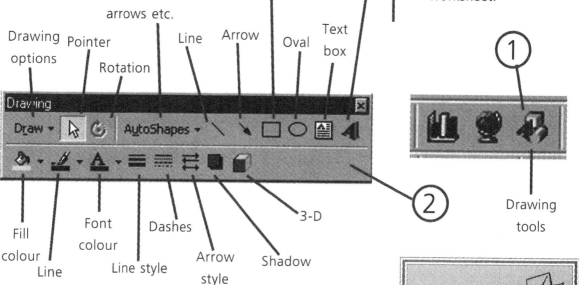

Connectors, arrows etc.

Rectangle

WordArt

Drawing options

Pointer

Rotation

Line

Arrow

Oval

Text box

Draw ▾

AutoShapes ▾

Fill colour

Line colour

Font colour

Line style

Dashes

Arrow style

Shadow

3-D

Drawing tools

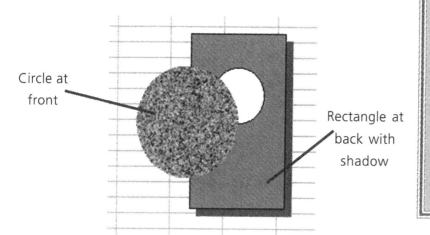

Circle at front

Rectangle at back with shadow

Tip

To draw a perfect circle or square, select the ellipse or rectangle and then hold down the [Shift] key while you mark out the shape.

Options

- To move an object, click on it and then drag it to a new position.

- To delete an object, click on it and then press **[Delete]**.

Graphic objects can be moved, resized and deleted. You can also change the colour or background pattern for an object by selecting from the palette on the Drawing toolbox.

Two or more objects can be grouped together by holding down the **[Shift]** key and clicking on them, then clicking on Group in the Draw options. When objects are in a group, they are treated as a single object for the purposes of moving them, changing the colour and pattern, and so on. To make the objects independent again, click on an object in the group and then on Ungroup in the Draw options.

Tip

The arrow and text box are particularly useful for adding comments to charts.

Take note

Like all Excel toolbars, the Drawing toolbar can be dragged from its default position above the status bar onto the sheet itself. It can also be resized.

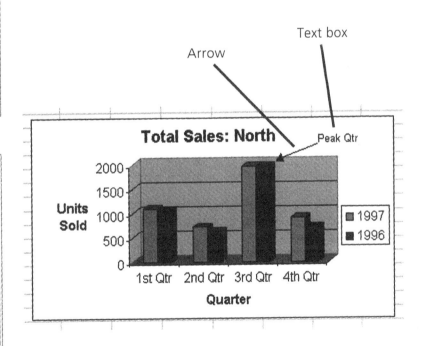

Text boxes

Although you can add text to a worksheet by typing into a cell, there are occasions when it is useful to have a more flexible approach. The use of text boxes lets you add any piece of text to the worksheet, at any position.

For example, you can add a heading as a text box, and apply to it any font and box format you like.

Since these boxes are independent of the main sheet, there is no effect on the underlying sheet. Therefore, you can have large headings or small annotations without the need to change the row heights to fit the text. This is useful if you want to add text to the side of other data, using a different point size.

Basic steps

To add a text box:

1 Click on the Text Box button in the Drawing toolbar.

2 Mark the area to be covered by the text box.

3 Enter the text.

Tip

Text boxes are also useful for annotating charts; you can add any piece of text at any point on a chart.

Text box

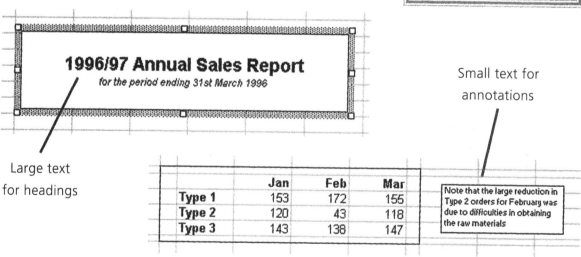

1996/97 Annual Sales Report
for the period ending 31st March 1996

Large text for headings

Small text for annotations

	Jan	Feb	Mar
Type 1	153	172	155
Type 2	120	43	118
Type 3	143	138	147

Note that the large reduction in Type 2 orders for February was due to difficulties in obtaining the raw materials

The text box and its contents can be edited in a variety of ways:

- Click on the box to select it. (It is given a grey border.) You can then apply a different pattern or colour to the background, or colour to the text.

- Drag the sides of the box to move it or the sizing handles to change its size.

- Click on the box again to edit the text. Any part of the text can be marked and have its typeface, size and attributes changed, in the same way as for text in a cell.

- The text can be left-aligned, centred or right-aligned.

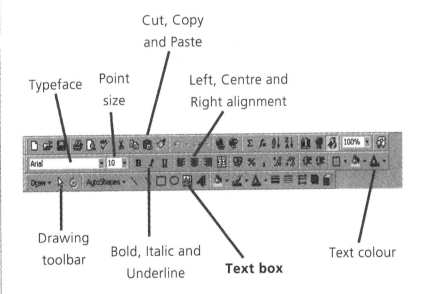

121

Summary of Section 12

- ❑ Any blocks of data can be represented by a chart or graph.

- ❑ Charts and graphs may be embedded on the worksheet or on separate chart sheets in the workbook.

- ❑ The Chart Wizard is a set of four dialogue boxes that determine the chart type and any text attached to it.

- ❑ Charts can be moved or resized; they do not affect the underlying data and formulae.

- ❑ Any change to the data results in a corresponding change to the chart.

- ❑ Graphic objects are added with the Drawing toolbar.

- ❑ Text boxes can be overlaid on any part of a worksheet or chart. Any typeface, size, attributes or colour can be used for any part of the text, without affecting the worksheet below.

13 Printing

Printer set-up

Traditionally, printing has always been the most fraught and unpredictable part of any computer process – and there is little point in going to the trouble of entering information on the computer if you cannot produce printed output. Fortunately, printing is one aspect of computer use that has become much easier with the advent of Windows 95. If you can produce output from one Windows 95 application, then you should be able to do so from any other.

The first stage is to check that Windows 95 is set up correctly for printing.

Basic steps

1 Select Settings in the Windows 95 Start menu and click on Printers.

2 Double-click on the icon for your most frequently used printer.

3 Click on Set As Default in the Printer menu to set the printer as the Windows 95 default.

4 Click on Properties in the Printer menu to change other default features (orientation, margins, scaling etc.)

Double-click to set up printer

Click here to set printer as default

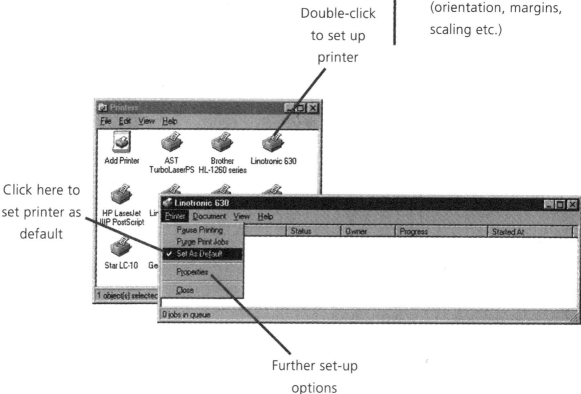

Further set-up options

Further options

- The **General** box allows you to enter comments, print an information page at the start of each print run (useful for networked printers) and print a test page.

- The **Details** box selects the printer port, printer driver and other hardware information.

- The **Paper** box lets you choose the paper tray (for printers with more than one), size of paper, orientation (which way round the paper is to be printed) and default number of copies.

- The **Graphics** box sets resolution and scaling.

- The remaining tabs set fonts, memory, printer instructions and other details.

The Properties option in the Printer menu leads to a box of set-up information. This has two or more tabs, each of which sets a number of printer options. All of these set defaults for each time you print but can be overridden on any particular print run.

The options that are provided vary, depending on the printer that has been selected.

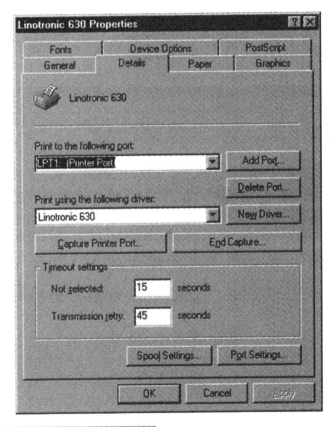

Tip

To print to a file rather than to the printer change Print To The Following Port in the Details box to FILE.

Page set-up

The Page Setup option in the Excel 97 File menu lets you determine the way in which a particular sheet will be printed. There are four sections, the first of which contains the Page settings:

- **Orientation** gives you either portrait (tall, thin) pages or landscape (pages printed sideways).

- **Scaling** is either a fixed percentage (e.g. 50% to reduce everything to half size) or the largest size possible for the sheets to fit the page. For best-fit scaling, choose the number of pages to be printed.

- **Paper size** provides a range of standard page sizes.

- **Print quality** is available only for some types of printer (e.g. draft and letter quality for some dot matrix printers).

- **First page number** determines the page number for the first page: AUTO defaults to 1, unless this print run follows on from another, in which case page numbering carries on from the previous run.

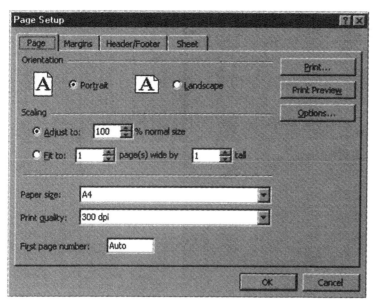

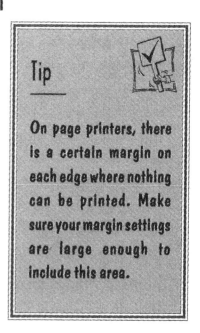

Tip

On page printers, there is a certain margin on each edge where nothing can be printed. Make sure your margin settings are large enough to include this area.

☐ The **Top** margin is the space above the main text area, including the space used by the header.

☐ The **Bottom** margin is the space below the text area, including any footer.

☐ The **Left** and **Right** margins are the spaces on either side.

☐ The **Header** and **Footer** settings determine the positions of the header and footer within the top and bottom margins (being the distance from the edge of the paper).

☐ The **Center on Page** options let you centre any sheet that does not fill the page. The sheet can be centred horizontally, vertically or both.

The Margins tab on the Page Setup box lets you decide how much blank space there should be at the top, bottom and sides of the sheet.

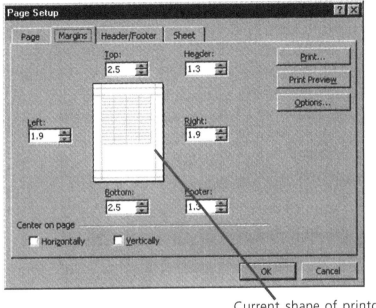

Current shape of printout

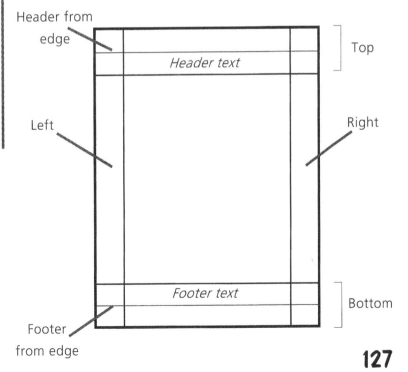

Headers and footers

You can choose a piece of text to be printed at the top and bottom of every page. The header and footer can cover several lines and each has three sections: for printing on the left or right or in the centre of the page.

A standard header/footer can be selected from the list, which offers defaults such as the sheet name, the filename, your name or your company name, and various combinations. Alternatively, you can create your own headers and footers by clicking on the Custom buttons. Each header/footer can contain any text (which can be formatted in the usual way) plus a variety of special codes: page number, total pages, current date, time, filename and worksheet name.

☐ The **Header** is a piece of text that is printed at the top of each page.

☐ The **Footer** is text that appears at the bottom of every page.

Page number

Total pages

Current date

Current time

Filename

Worksheet tab name

Buttons for special codes

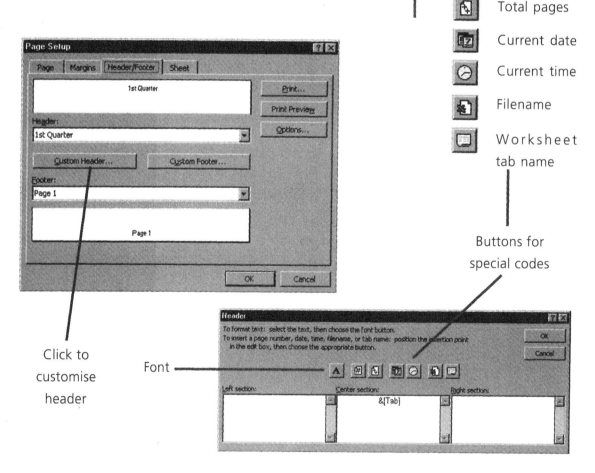

Click to customise header

Font

128

Options

- ☐ The **Print Area** is the default range to be printed.

- ☐ The **Print Titles** are rows and columns that are to be repeated on every page when the worksheet will not fit on one page.

- ☐ The **Print** options decide which optional features will be printed.

- ☐ The **Page Order** is used when the worksheet is both too long **and** too wide for one page; it decides whether printing is done from top to bottom and then left to right, or vice versa.

The final Page Setup tab determines the way in which the sheet itself is printed.

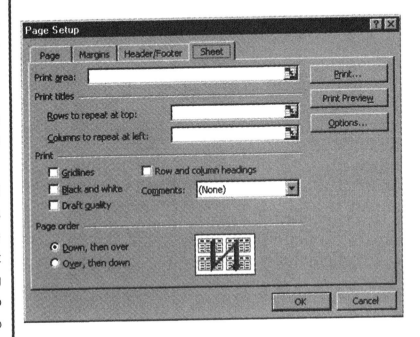

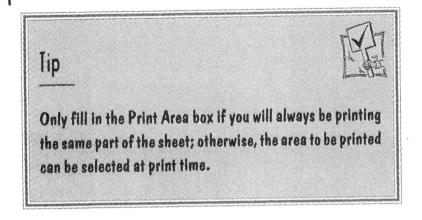

Tip

Only fill in the Print Area box if you will always be printing the same part of the sheet; otherwise, the area to be printed can be selected at print time.

Preview

The Print Preview option in the File menu lets you see on screen what the final printed page will look like. As well as zooming into or out of the display, there are options to take you directly to other printer activities (as a shortcut to the File menu).

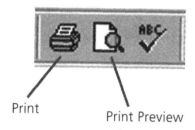

Print   Print Preview

Page as it will appear
when printed

Options

Next displays the next page.

Previous displays the previous page.

Zoom expands or contracts the display.

Print takes you to the File | Print options.

Setup loads Page Setup.

Margins lets you change the page margins.

Page Break Preview lets you see the page breaks and change them.

Close returns you to the worksheet.

Microsoft Excel - Sales 97 North Actual

Zoom | Print... | Setup... | Margins | Page Break Preview | Close | Help

Summary

1896/97 Annual Sales Report

TOTAL SALES: NORTH

Total Sales: North

Page 1

Preview: Page 1 of 1   NUM

Print options

The information to be printed is chosen from:

- **Selection**: the part of the worksheet previously marked by dragging the pointer over a range

- **Active Sheet(s)**: those sheets whose tabs are currently selected

- **Entire Workbook**: all sheets

You can limit the amount printed by selecting a range of pages, rather than **All**.

You can also specify the number of copies to print.

Once all the set-up work has been completed (and this is something you should only have to do once for each workbook), you can start printing. The File | Print command has a very simple dialogue box although, in common with the other print commands, it has buttons to take you to other set-up stages.

Printer
properties

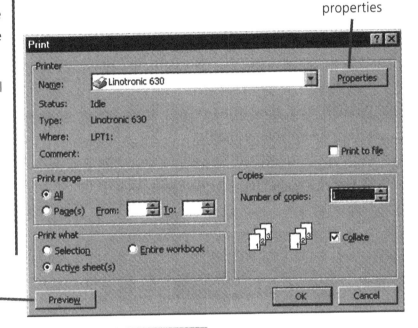

Page
preview

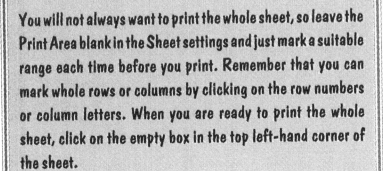

Tip

You will not always want to print the whole sheet, so leave the Print Area blank in the Sheet settings and just mark a suitable range each time before you print. Remember that you can mark whole rows or columns by clicking on the row numbers or column letters. When you are ready to print the whole sheet, click on the empty box in the top left-hand corner of the sheet.

Summary of Section 13

❏ Printing is controlled by Windows 95 and its Printers folder.

❏ The Excel 97 Page Setup lets you decide details of page layout, margins, headers and footers, and area to be printed.

❏ Headers are lines of text printed at the top of each page; footers are printed at the bottom of the page.

❏ Headers and footers can include special codes for page number, total pages, current date and time, filename and worksheet name.

❏ Print Preview allows you to see on screen what the page will look like when printed.

❏ You can print the entire workbook, a selection of sheets or just the range that is currently selected.

14 Advanced features

Sorting data

The basic principles for using Excel 97 have now been covered. However, Excel contains many more facilities, some extremely useful, others rather obscure. This final section looks at a few of the additional features on offer.

Sorting data is one of the easiest tasks and has many uses. Simple sorting involves marking a range and then clicking on one of the sort buttons, to sort the contents of the cells in either ascending (A to Z) or descending (Z to A) order.

Ascending order
(A to Z)

Descending order
(Z to A)

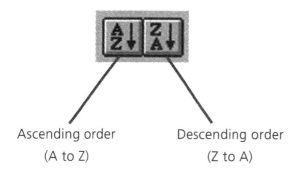

Unsorted

Albert	-623
(also)	0.999
--- ends ---	3.14159
aardvark	78
125 train	128
{yes}	--- ends ---
A	(also)
Beethoven	{yes}
33 rpm	125 train
beetroot	33 rpm
128	A
78	aardvark
3.14159	Albert
-623	Beethoven
0.999	beetroot

Sorted

Rules

□ All numeric values come before text values and are sorted in order of magnitude.

□ Numbers entered as text are sorted character by character (so '12' is before '3', because the character '1' comes before '3').

□ Characters other than numbers and letters are first in the sort order, followed by numeric characters and then alphabetic letters.

□ Upper and lower case letters are treated the same, unless you specify otherwise.

Basic steps

1 Select Sort from the Data menu.

2 Choose the columns on which the sort is to be based (selecting from the list of currently highlighted columns).

3 For each sort column, choose Ascending or Descending order.

4 Specify whether or not there is a header row.

5 Click on the Options buttons to further refine the sort.

For a more sophisticated sort, select Sort from the Data menu. This allows you to choose up to three columns for sorting. If the entries in the first sort column are the same, the sort is based on the second column; if these are also identical, the order is determined by the third column.

You can choose ascending or descending order for each column independently, and also make the sort case-sensitive (with capitals before lower case letters).

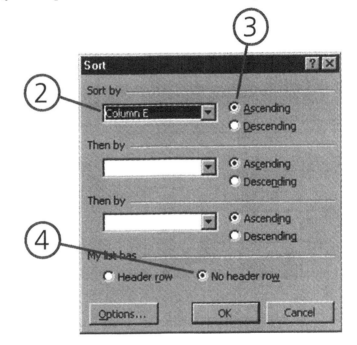

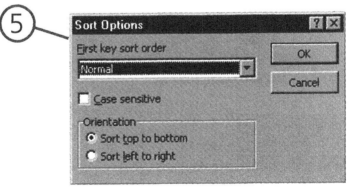

Find and replace

The Find option in the Edit Menu searches the worksheet for a specified piece of text. This may be a word, a phrase or just a few characters from a word. The search will be in formulae and values, unless you specify **Values** (in which case formulae are ignored). The search is in the whole worksheet, unless you have marked a range or selected a group of worksheets.

The Replace option searches for one piece of text and then replaces it with another one.

Wildcards

Two wildcards can be used in the Find command:

- ❑ ? represents any single character.

- ❑ * represents any group of characters.

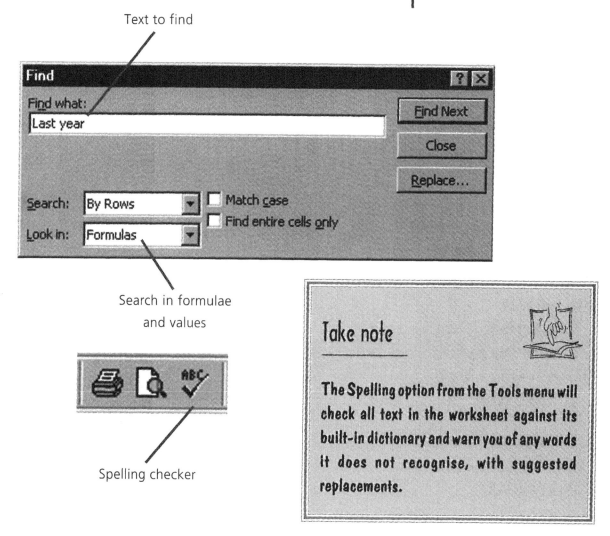

Text to find

Search in formulae and values

Spelling checker

Take note

The Spelling option from the Tools menu will check all text in the worksheet against its built-in dictionary and warn you of any words it does not recognise, with suggested replacements.

Basic steps

To create a new toolbar:

1 Select View I Toolbars.

2 Click on Customize.

3 Click on the New button.

4 Click on the Commands tab.

5 Select a Category.

6 Drag an icon to the toolbar.

Repeat steps 5 and 6 until the toolbar is complete, then click on Close.

Toolbars

Excel is equipped with a number of toolbars, which can be customised to suit your own preferences. The View I Toolbars command lists the toolbars. Clicking on any of the boxes next to the bars turns them on or off.

To change the contents of the toolbars, click on Customize:

● New buttons are added to the toolbars by dragging the buttons from the Commands tab of the dialogue box to the toolbars.

● Buttons are removed from toolbars by clicking on them (on the toolbars, not the dialogue box) and pressing **[Delete]**.

● Clicking on the New button creates a new toolbar.

Defaults

Available toolbars

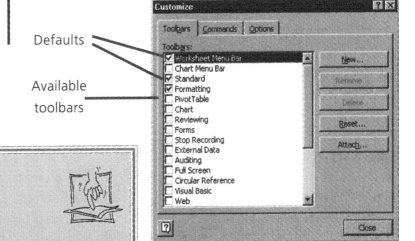

Take note

Toolbars are added as separate windows but if you drag them into the toolbar area at the top of the screen, they lose their control menus and titles. Similarly, dragging any toolbar (including the default toolbars) into the main sheet converts it into a window.

Custom toolbar

Comments

Data can be annotated by attaching a comment to any cell. The comment takes the form of a piece of text entered into a dialogue box, using Insert | Comment. All the usual editing facilities are available. Comments are saved with the worksheet.

The comment attached to a cell is displayed if you pause with the pointer over the cell. All comments for the worksheet can be viewed with View | Comments and any one can be edited or deleted.

The Comments toolbar provides viewing and editing facilities.

Basic steps

To add a comment:

1 Click on a cell.

2 Select Insert | Comment.

3 Type the text into the comment box.

4 Click on Close.

A red triangle in the top right-hand corner of the cell indicates that a comment is attached.

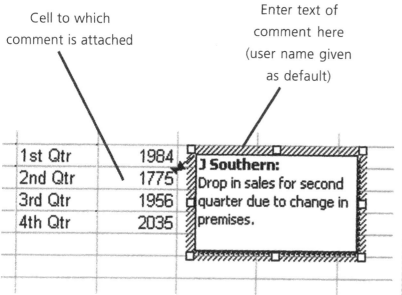

Cell to which comment is attached

Enter text of comment here (user name given as default)

1st Qtr	1984
2nd Qtr	1775
3rd Qtr	1956
4th Qtr	2035

J Southern:
Drop in sales for second quarter due to change in premises.

Comments toolbar

Tip

To provide easy access to comments, add the New Comment button to one of the toolbars. This button can be found in the Insert category and is a shortcut to Insert|Comment.

New Comment button

Basic steps

1 Select From File from the Insert | Picture sub-menu.

2 Open the folder containing the picture file.

3 Click on the filename.

4 Click on OK.

Adding pictures

Bitmaps, Windows metafiles and other pictures can be added to the Excel worksheets, as illustrations or to enhance the appearance of the finished sheet. For example, you could create a company logo in Paint and then add this to the top of all your reports.

Pictures are added with the Insert | Picture menu. In the same way as text boxes, charts and graphic objects, pictures are overlaid on the sheet and have no effect on the underlying data and formulae.

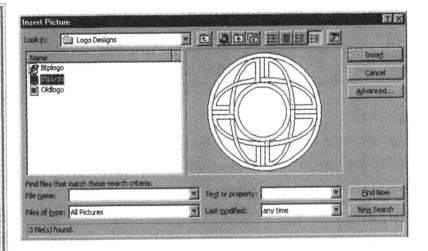

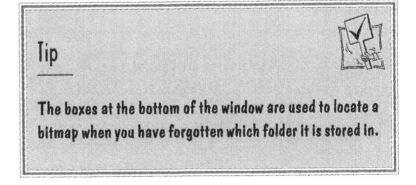

Macros

A **macro** is a way of automating a series of frequently-needed actions. At its simplest, a macro is created by recording a series of actions which are then replayed.

Valid Excel name

Optional description

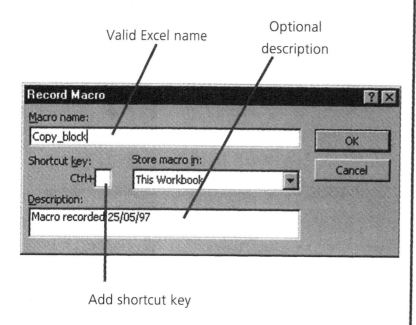

Add shortcut key

To record a macro:

1 Select Tools | Macro and click on Record New Macro.

2 Enter a name for the macro and description. The name must be a valid Excel name (letters, numbers, underscore; no spaces).

3 If required, type a letter to be used with **[Ctrl]** as a shortcut to the macro.

4 Click on OK.

5 Any actions you now take are recorded, including any mistakes you make!

6 When you have finished, click on the Stop button.

Take note

By default, all cell references are absolute; i.e. the same cells will be used regardless of which cell is current when the macro is run. For the macro to perform its actions relative to the start position, click on the Relative References button.

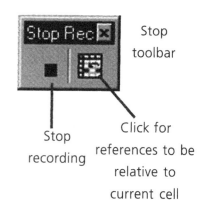

Stop toolbar

Stop recording

Click for references to be relative to current cell

140

Buttons

The Macro box has the following buttons:

- **Run** runs the macro.

- **Cancel** returns you to the worksheet.

- **Step Into** runs the macro one step at a time, so you can see how it works and detect bugs.

- **Edit** allows you to change the macro.

- **Create** lets you write a new macro (available when you enter a new Macro Name.)

- **Delete** permanently deletes the macro.

- **Options** lets you change the shortcut key and description.

There are several ways to run the macro:

- Select Macro from the Tools menu, click on the macro name and click on Run.

- If the macro was given a shortcut key, use that without selecting any menu option.

- The macro can be added to a toolbar or menu (see page 142).

You can also add a button to the worksheet and attach a macro to it (see page 143).

Existing macros

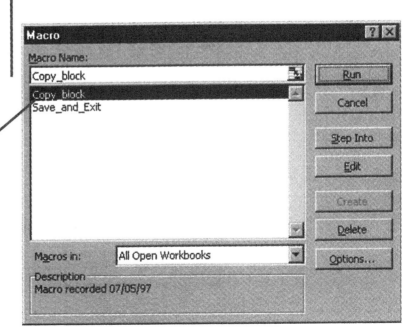

Editing a macro

Macros are written and edited in the Visual Basic programming language. When you record a macro, Excel creates a Visual Basic procedure containing the necessary code. This code can be edited and new lines can be added. The Visual Basic code is stored in a separate area of the workbook, by default named **Module1**.

To edit a macro, Select Tools | Macro | Macros, click on the macro name and then on Edit.

Full details of Visual Basic procedures are given in the on-line help. (If Visual Basic on-line help was not included in the installation process, it can be added by re-running the Setup program.) Select 'Contents and Index' from the Help menu and choose Microsoft Excel Visual Basic Reference from the Contents tab.

To add a macro to a toolbar or menu:

1 Select Tools | Customize.

2 Click on the Commands tab and the Macros category.

3 Drag the Custom Button to a toolbar or the Custom Menu Item to the menu bar.

4 Click on the Modify Selection button in the Customize box and then on Assign Macro. Click on a macro and then on OK.

5 Click on Modify Selection again. For a custom button, use Change Button Image to choose a new bitmap. For a menu item, type a new title in the Name box (including an & in front of the letter to be used as a shortcut).

Clicking on the new toolbar button or menu item will now activate the selected macro.

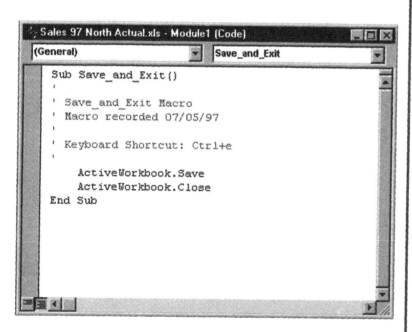

```
Sales 97 North Actual.xls - Module1 (Code)
(General)                    Save_and_Exit
Sub Save_and_Exit()
'
' Save_and_Exit Macro
' Macro recorded 07/05/97
'
' Keyboard Shortcut: Ctrl+e
'
    ActiveWorkbook.Save
    ActiveWorkbook.Close
End Sub
```

Basic steps

To add a button to the worksheet:

1 Display the Forms toolbar by selecting View | Toolbars and clicking on Forms.

2 Click on the button icon.

3 Mark out the position for the button.

4 Assign a macro to the button by selecting from the macro list.

5 Edit the button name (click on the button text and then replace it with a more suitable name).

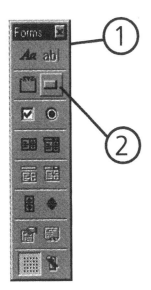

Although macros speed up frequently-used operations, the use of the Tools menu is not particularly convenient. Adding a command button to the sheet is a very simple process. A macro is attached to the button and then, to run the macro, all you have to do is click on the button. This is a particularly useful approach when setting up macros for other people to use.

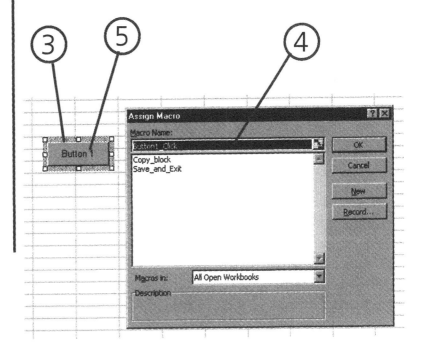

Tip

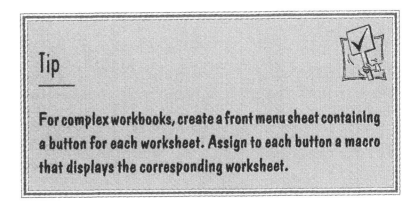

For complex workbooks, create a front menu sheet containing a button for each worksheet. Assign to each button a macro that displays the corresponding worksheet.

Summary of Section 14

❑ Data can be sorted into either ascending or descending order; the sort may be based on one or more columns and can be made case-sensitive.

❑ The Find and Replace options allow you to search for text or replace one text string with another throughout the worksheet.

❑ The toolbars can be customised and new toolbars can be created with any selection of buttons.

❑ Comments can be added to any cell with Insert | Comment.

❑ Bitmaps and other graphics can be overlaid on a worksheet using Insert | Picture.

❑ Macros are used to replay frequently-used command sequences or to provide more complex control over worksheet activities.

❑ Macros are written in the Visual Basic programming language and are stored in a separate module.

❑ Command buttons can be added to worksheets and a macro is associated with each button.

Index

149

Transparencies, 116
Trigonometry functions, 42
Typeface, 84

U

Undo options, 17

V

View | Toolbars, 137
Visual Basic, 142

W

Width of columns, 72
Window size, 4
Window | Freeze Panes, 80
Window | New Window, 98
Windows
 changing, 23
 multiple, 98
Workbooks, 94
 printing, 131

Worksheets, 6
 automating, 140
 closing, 24
 copying, 101
 deleting, 100
 grouping, 99
 inserting, 100
 loading, 25
 moving, 101
 moving around, 7
 multiple, 94
 new, 96
 printing, 131
 renaming, 22, 95
 saving, 20
 windows, 23

X

XLS extension, 21